KEYS TO PARENTING YOUR FIVE YEAR OLD

Marti White, Ph.D.

BARRON'S

Cover photo by Scott Barrow, Inc., Cold Spring, NY

All inquiries should be addressed to:
Barron's Educational Series, Inc.
250 Wireless Boulevard
Hauppauge, New York 11788

Library of Congress Catalog Card No.: 95-18025

International Standard Book No. 0-8120-9366-6

Library of Congress Cataloging-in-Publication Data

White, Marti, 1954–
    Keys to parenting your five year old / Marti White.
        p. cm.
    Includes bibliographical references (p. –) and index.
    ISBN 0-8120-9366-6
    1. Child rearing.   2. Parenting.   I. Title.
    HQ769.W517   1995
    649′.123—dc20   95-18025
                                                                CIP

PRINTED IN THE UNITED STATES OF AMERICA

5678   8800   987654321

CONTENTS

INTRODUCTION

Your child has reached the age of five and is now making the transition from "preschool" to "childhood." He or she is now quite self-dependent in many routines at home, and the ongoing developmental changes that occurred so rapidly from birth to age four now begin to slow. By the age of five most children are great talkers. They are developing the skills that prepare them for school and have started to develop the interpersonal skills that help them to play well with other children. Although the developmental changes are not as apparent at age five as they were when your child first started to walk or talk, your child continues to grow in all areas.

The goal of this book is to provide some guidelines to help you as parents know what to expect from your five year old, as well as give suggestions on how to handle the unique changes that occur at this age. In Part One, Your Five Year Old's Development, the focus is on your child's capabilities. Cognitive, language, motor, and social and emotional development are discussed. It is important to realize as you read this section that these descriptions are provided as guidelines. Each child is a unique individual who develops at his or her own pace. Each of us displays individual strengths and weaknesses, and it is important to remember that all children are different.

Part Two, Your Child's Personality, talks about many issues and concerns that arise as your child becomes more independent. Five year olds are often confusing to parents as they make the transition from being rambunctious, dependent four year olds to cooperative, self-reliant individuals. As your child attempts to master new tasks, his or her level of frustration may become overwhelming and, at times, almost impossible. Personality factors play an important role in the way you and your child deal with this new stage.

Part Three provides some suggestions on how to foster your child's development in different areas. As children approach the age of five, their dependence on parents starts to diminish as they develop the capability to complete many tasks themselves. Although it is often difficult for parents to come to terms with the fact that their "baby" is growing up, it is important to realize that giving children responsibilities and allowing them to do things for themselves will help them develop into self-sufficient young adults. Suggestions for disciplining your five year old are also given in this section. As your child grows and develops different skills, the demands for addressing different behavior also change.

Finally, the joys and concerns about the start of school are discussed. Most five-year-old children will be entering kindergarten. This may or may not be their first school experience, and with it come many questions and concerns. Such issues as determining whether your child is ready for school, what to expect from your first teacher conference, and how to foster reading and writing skills are addressed in this section.

Young children are complex people whose skills and abilities are often interrelated. It is certainly reasonable to read sections of this book to gain information about a specific area. It is suggested, however, that the whole book be read so that you can get an overview of your child's capabilities and needs.

1

COGNITIVE DEVELOPMENT

Cognitive development is the process by which we gain knowledge and become thinking beings. It includes a range of skills necessary for organizing and understanding our experiences with the world. When children are born, their ability to interact with the environment is limited to making their basic needs known through crying. As they develop motor control, infants becomes more capable of picking up objects, playing with toys, and, sometimes, expressing unhappiness by throwing things! The emergence of language allows children to develop ongoing interactions with the environment. These interactions result in the acquisition of numerous skills, which range from labeling objects to expressing thoughts and feelings in a coherent fashion. By the age of five, children are extremely capable people. As their attention span increases, so does the quality of their experiences with the environment.

How do these skills develop? Experience, encouragement, affection, and stimulation from the environment help children develop their thought processes. They begin to understand concepts or the commonalities among different objects. A green square, a green circle, and a green triangle, once categorized only by color, can now be categorized as either shapes or by color.

Children also begin to use words and symbols to solve tasks and problems. The understanding that a symbol actually represents something else is important for the development of mathematics and language skills.

Memory, the ability to recall and respond to events over a period of time, is another important area in cognitive development. As memory skills increase, children are able to hold onto information they learned at one point in time and use it as a building block for future learning.

This process of cognitive development has taken your child from a helpless, crying infant to the talkative, capable little person you see at age five.

What are some of the specific cognitive skills your child may display at this time? By the age of five, children have started to learn colors and are generally able to name eight of them. They are able to identify the shapes that they have learned from day-to-day experiences.

Many five year olds are able to count by rote to 20 and start to develop *one-to-one number correspondence*, the understanding that numbers are symbols that have meaning. When you ask for 3 forks, your child is now able to count out 3 forks on a consistent basis. They understand the concept of *how many* and are able to count 10 or more objects.

Experiences with the environment enable children to identify and sort objects according to texture, such as rough or smooth, soft or hard, and wet or dry. Through repetition and a general interest in written words, many five year olds are able to recognize their own printed name and can match letters and numbers. Five year olds are able to identify such concepts as first, middle, and last. They can demonstrate an understanding of *beside*, *behind*, and *next to* and can follow a series of three directions. Many children are able to tell their address and can draw a picture of a person with anywhere from two to six parts.

As children continue to grow and develop, new skills begin to emerge. Between the ages of five and six, number concepts continue to improve. They are now able to count up to 20 objects and name 10 numerals. Some children begin to perform simple calculations within 5 as they start to understand the relationship between the number 5 and the fingers they have on one hand. Sequencing skills continue to improve, as does the ability to count by rote. Many children can now tell what number comes next. An interest in money concepts brings about the ability to recognize coins. The understanding that each coin represents a quantity is beginning to develop, and later in the year, most children are able to identify a penny, nickel, dime, and quarter.

Recognition of uppercase and lowercase letters and the beginning of a small *sight-word vocabulary* (words recognized on sight) also occurs during this time. Many children at this age level are able to tell the days of the week in order and understand the concepts of *some, many,* and *several.*

Eye-hand coordination improves during this time, and many five year olds are now able to print their first name in uppercase letters. Drawings improve in quality, and pictures of people are more elaborate and contain approximately eight parts.

The ability to distinguish right from left also emerges at this time. Children often practice these skills by asking which way you are turning when you drive or on which side a particular building is located.

There is a noticeable increase in attention span during this year, and children are now able to spend 12 to 15 minutes with a toy or activity.

A word of caution is suggested as you compare your child's skill levels with those just described. These descriptions are provided as guidelines to give a general idea of the types of skills you can expect from your child. Each child develops at his or her own pace. If your child includes only five parts on a picture of a person or can only identify a penny, do not panic. These skills may be emerging at a slightly slower pace and, with time, will become a solid part of your child's repertoire.

Children also display areas of strength and weakness in their development. Some five year olds may be ready to print their first and last names but may be very unsure of number concepts. Other children may be quite adept with counting skills but be hesitant in their ability to identify letters. When looking at your child's skills, keep in mind that each of us has strengths and weaknesses, as well as likes and dislikes, that affect our performance in specific areas.

2

~~~~~~

SPEECH AND LANGUAGE DEVELOPMENT

I f you haven't yet noticed, most five year olds love to talk! An hour-long car trip can be delightful or seem like an eternity if you happen to have a chatty five year old with you.

There are noticeable changes in the language of five-year-old children, particularly in the relevance and conciseness of their verbalizations. Their answers to questions are more succinct and direct. The questions your five year old asks are more relevant and are aimed at gaining information. Language skills are characterized by the use of basic grammatical structures, such as plurals, conjunctions, and verb tenses (past, present, and future). Your five year old is now able to take appropriate turns in conversations with both peers and adults. With a vocabulary of 2,500 or more words, your five year old now demonstrates an inner logic in language as well as an ability to categorize.

Receptive Language

Receptive language, the ability to understand what is said, is now well developed. Your five year old can follow directions consisting of three steps. "Please put your shoes in your room, hang up your coat, and wash your hands" are directions many five year olds are able to follow. Verbal directions are incorporated into play skills, and there is an understanding of some abstract concepts. Your child has an understanding of spatial relations, such as *on*, *behind*, *under*, and *in back*. Most five year olds can understand the concepts of *same* and *different* and can show you a penny, nickel, and dime.

Expressive Language

Expressive language skills, the ability to use spoken words to express thoughts, are characterized by the use of sentences containing six or more words. Five-year-old children are able to describe things by using conjunctions to string together words and phrases. They are able to respond appropriately to social greetings, such as "Hi, how are you?" and use language to regulate social interactions with others.

They are able to define objects by their use and can tell what things are made of. By this age, most children should know their address and are able to carry a plot in a story. For example, when telling a story about Halloween and ghosts, they are able to maintain the same story line from start to finish without wandering off the topic.

Stimulating Language Development

Language skills can be stimulated by encouraging your child to use language to express feelings, ideas, wishes, and fears. Instead of asking a direct question, commenting on what your child did or how you think your child feels will stimulate more speech. "What did you do in school today?" will generate more conversation than "Did you have a good day at school?", which can be answered with a simple yes or no. Asking a child to explain how he or she did something will generate speech more than a simple comment, such as "I really like that picture you drew."

Allow opportunities for your child to learn songs, rhymes, or verses from memory, and continue to read longer stories. As your child's attention span and memory skills increase, longer and more complex books and stories will help foster language development. Listen to your child when she talks to you, and avoid using baby language when you speak to her. Remember that children understand more than they are able to say. This is important to keep in mind when you are having conversations that your child should not overhear!

Speech Concerns

There are two areas of speech and language development that sometimes become areas of concern for parents. Speech sound development, sometimes referred to as articulation or phonological development, can have an impact on a child's ability to speak clearly. Speech sounds develop as your child grows. By age three, most children should be 75 percent intelligible to strangers. By age four, their speech should be 90 percent intelligible to strangers. Some sounds (*t, v, l, th, j, z,* and *zh*) do not develop until six or seven years of age.

To help your child speak more clearly, be a good speech model. Pronounce words clearly, slowly, and correctly. Use new words and sounds often in your conversation with your child so she has opportunities to hear them.

Speech dysfluency, or stuttering, is another area of concern for some parents. Between the ages of two and six, many children begin to repeat sounds, syllables, or whole words while they are speaking. This is considered a normal, nonfluent duplication of speech. An episode of dysfluency may last for several weeks or months and may disappear for a time only to reappear later.

Acceptance of your child's speech pattern by not calling attention to the repetitions is very important. Do not tell your child to slow down or take a breath. This is often difficult to do when you want to help your child get the words out, but it is very important to give her plenty of time to talk without being interrupted.

Be sure your child is getting enough rest and exercise and that she has an appropriate diet. Relieving any tensions at home can also help if your child is showing signs of dysfluency.

When do these dysfluencies change from typical development to an area of concern? True stuttering affects only one to four percent of all children. If you see your child develop "secondary characteristics," it may be time to consult a professional. Secondary characteristics consist of such behaviors as twitching, facial grimaces, avoiding eye contact when talking, or leg and arm movements. These behaviors usually indicate that the child is aware of the dysfluency and is struggling to overcome the blocks in speech. If your child's speech dysfluency lasts for longer than eight weeks or you are concerned that it may progress to something more serious, contact a speech and language pathologist who has specific training in dysfluency therapy. A specialist in the field can tell you if it is something to concerned about or simply part of your child's normal developmental pattern.

Speech and language difficulties can often be remediated by a speech and language therapist. For most children, delays in these areas respond to a period of therapy and, in many cases, do not have an effect on overall development or performance in school.

3

∿∿∿∿∿∿∿∿∿∿∿∿∿∿∿∿∿∿∿∿∿∿∿∿∿∿∿∿∿∿∿∿∿

MOTOR
DEVELOPMENT

Tricycles, roller skates, jumping, climbing, skipping, and swinging are only some of the activities that consume the days of five year olds. Given a choice, most children would rather be outside, engaged in some of these activities, rather than sitting inside playing a game. Five year olds are more poised and display better gross motor control than fine motor control.

Gross Motor Skills

Gross motor skills, the use of large muscles, are becoming well developed by age five. By this age, children become more restrained and less active in their overall level of movement. Your five year old is able to walk backward, placing one foot directly behind the other, and can run on his tiptoes. Stairs become an easy obstacle to overcome as he goes up and down stairs, alternating feet. For most five year olds, pedaling a tricycle has also become an easy task. Some well-coordinated children may even be ready for a two-wheeler with training wheels at this age. Climbing is done with sureness, and you can be certain there will be ripped pants or dirty knees from all the outside activities. Five-year-old children are able to turn somersaults and can jump from a 12 inch landing on their toes. A five to six year old can walk on a balance beam and may show a genuine interest in roller skates or in-line skates. Remember that knee pads, elbow pads, and a helmet are essential accessories to avoid injury.

Fine Motor Skills

Fine motor skills, such as those that involve manipulating objects, eye-hand coordination, and perceptual skills, are also developing at this age. These skills generally develop at a slightly slower pace than gross motor skills. Boys may be less adept than girls at this point but eventually reach the same level. Your five year old is able to build with blocks, manipulate buttons, and tie shoelaces. Coloring within the lines and cutting and pasting skills are emerging but are not well developed. Your child may be able to trace a triangle and copy a cross and square. Most children can cut on a straight line and can print their first name in capital letters. As children approach their sixth birthday, these skills become more refined. They can now copy a triangle, write the numbers 1 to 5, and color within the lines. Scissor use improves, and they are now able to cut out simple shapes. Handedness is well established by the time children reach their sixth birthday.

Fostering Motor Development

How can you, as parents, help your child's motor development? First, engage your child in any kind of physical activity to improve coordination. Running, jumping, and throwing a ball will all strengthen your child's gross motor development. Provide your child with the opportunity to engage in various fine motor activities. Children who have difficulty with fine motor coordination are reluctant to engage in tasks that require those skills. Using special markers, pencils, or crayons can sometimes entice a child to engage in drawing tasks. Allowing your child to "help" Mom or Dad cut out grocery coupons is a good way to improve scissor use. Clay and play dough, as messy as they can be, are great tools for strengthening hand muscles.

Sometimes, taking a close look around your house and observing the kinds of activities your child is interested in helps provide ideas for fostering fine and gross motor skills. A few more suggestions follow:

- Use clothespins to hang small articles of clothing on the line.
- Sort dried beans.
- Hammer nails (with supervision!) to develop eye-hand coordination.
- Seal and unseal the lids from plastic containers.
- Set up an obstacle course using chairs, boxes, and other household items to help improve gross motor development.

4

~~~~~~

SOCIAL DEVELOPMENT

Most five-year-old children view family life at home as the center of their world. The primary caretaker, who is often Mom, is the focus of most activities. They like to please Mom, do things with her, and, generally, just be around her. Although five year olds are strongly connected to Mom, their relationship with Dad is generally pleasant. They look forward to and get great enjoyment out of special occasions with Dad.

At five years of age your child may have strong feelings for the family as a whole and especially enjoys celebrations, such as birthday parties and holidays. Relationships with grandparents are important at this age, especially if they live nearby and have frequent contact. Children this age are able to play reasonably well with younger siblings, and girls, especially, tend to be more protective, kind, and motherly. Typical episodes of teasing and taking toys are often seen when children are alone with their younger siblings.

Play skills with other children are fairly well developed at this age. Children often show a preference for playing outdoors. Cooperative play is generally limited to three children: more than three can be a source of conflict. As children learn to coordinate activities, true interaction and cooperation can happen. Between the ages of five and six, children begin to choose their own friends. They can engage in cooperative play with other children and play competitive games. Play takes on purpose and direction at this age. Games become more complicated, and social traits, such as leadership, aggression, and cooperation, become more apparent. Conflicts arise over who likes whom, who will play with whom, and who will be included or excluded. As a rule, friends change quickly among five year olds. Girls get into more verbal conflicts; boys tend to be more physical.

Boys and girls are generally able to play well together, although at this age there is often an interest in exploring sex differences. Children may play doctor to compare themselves to children of the same sex or to learn what the opposite sex looks like under their clothing. Parents should not overreact to this but attempt to redirect play to a more appropriate activity. Later, when you are alone with your child, a discussion of the differences between boys and girls is helpful. You should also include a discussion of body parts, emphasizing that there are public parts of our bodies that are okay for other people to see and private parts of our bodies that aren't okay for others to see. Follow your child's lead for the amount of information you need to provide. Some children are satisfied with very little information, and others have more questions and want more details. The important thing to remember is that your child's behavior is based on normal curiosity.

Five-year-old children are often very content with their world. They live very much in the here and now and like to please the people around them. They generally behave and, at five, are usually truthful.

Five year olds can have difficulty differentiating between right and wrong, however, and "lying" usually occurs for very specific reasons. Many of the lies told by five year olds are to gain attention from the adults around them. If there is something going on at home that is occupying your attention, telling a lie may be your child's way of redirecting that attention back to her.

Children around this age may also tell lies as a way of gaining parental approval. If your child feels she has done something that is not up to your standard, a lie can often seem like a good way of avoiding your response.

Fear of punishment is the third common reason for lies at this age level. If a child is concerned about harsh discipline, it may be time to reevaluate your discipline techniques. Make sure the punishment fits the crime, and remember that there is no clear distinction between right and wrong at this age. Five year olds have great imaginations, which may sometimes be mistaken for lying.

Finally, as parents, it is important to avoid double standards. Children who hear Mom tell a phone caller that Dad is not home (while he is sitting at the table) won't understand why they are being punished for doing the same thing Mom does!

5

EMOTIONAL DEVELOPMENT

S erious, *realistic*, and *literal* are all words that can be used to describe the emotional manner of your five year old. Patterns of friendly, cooperative, helpful behavior are characteristic of your child at this age. This is truly the focal age of good adjustment. There is very little moodiness at this time, and your five year old is not typically aggressive. He may cry if tired or angry and may stamp his feet or slam a door when frustrated. The tantrums seen at age five usually erupt over the conflict between what he wants to do and his actual skill level.

Emotions, such feelings as happiness, sadness, anger, love, frustration, and jealousy, are for most adults relatively easy to identify and label. Five-year-old children, however, can be frightened and overwhelmed by negative feelings. They may not be able to identify what they are feeling or know how to express these feelings appropriately.

You can help your child by confirming what you think your child is feeling and by suggesting ways to deal with that feeling. When your child tells you that his best friend chose to play with someone else at school, listen carefully to the details he provides. Validate his feelings with something like, "It sounds like you're feeling pretty angry that Tommy didn't play with you today."

Even when children are able to recognize emotions, they are not necessarily able to control them. Helping your child to identify and negotiate solutions to emotional situations will also help him to gain control over his emotions. In the previous example, you can help your child to generate several alternatives, such as finding another friend to play with, talking to Tommy about why he wouldn't play, or releasing his anger through some physical activity, such as riding his bike.

To assist your child in dealing with difficult situations, break challenges into small parts. As adults, we are often able to do this automatically for ourselves. Children need help in seeing that the overwhelming situation is actually made up of small, manageable parts. Your child's frustration when asked to pick up his toys may be caused by the overwhelming nature of the task, especially if there are toys all over the floor! Breaking down the task into small parts (first pick up the cars, then the puzzles, then the crayons, and so on) may relieve some of the frustration he is feeling.

Setting limits for your child will provide him with a good sense of security and guidance. Children know they are loved when Mom and Dad put some limits on their behavior. Let your child know what is acceptable behavior and what is not acceptable. "It's okay to punch a pillow when you are angry, but it's not okay to throw a toy across the room." "You can use your words to tell me you are angry, but you may not hit or kick."

Good emotional health starts with the ability to recognize and express the emotions that are a part of life. When your child expresses an emotion such as anger, help him learn to express the feeling by asking questions, such as: "What do you do when you are angry?" "What happens when you act a certain way?" and "How do other people react when they are angry?"

Sometimes children (and adults) experience several feelings at the same time. For a young child who is just learning to identify feelings, this can be both confusing and uncomfortable. Encourage your child to express his thoughts and help him identify the different feelings with statements such as "It sounds as if you're feeling pretty angry and sad at the same time." This may help alleviate some confusion and lets your child know that it is okay and appropriate to have several feelings at the same time.

If your child has difficulty labeling emotions, activities such as a feeling box or a feeling book can help foster this skill. To make a feeling box, use an old tissue box and pieces of paper. Write a different feeling on each piece of paper and place them in the box. Have your child pick out a paper, talk about the feeling, and draw a picture of a face to express that feeling. In a feeling book, your child can draw pictures that express different emotions. Start with the statement "I feel happy (substitute other emotions) when . . . " Allow your child to describe different circumstances and then draw the picture.

Finally, reinforce good choices. Be sure to verbally reinforce situations when your child is able to appropriately express an emotion without losing control. "I see how angry you are and you still remembered to use your words." This lets your child know that emotions are a normal part of life but that he has control over how those emotions are expressed.

6

MORAL DEVELOPMENT

By the age of five years, many children are able to begin to imagine themselves in the place of someone who is upset, and they feel bad for that person. This is the beginning of the development of empathetic thinking. Consistent with most other behaviors, how parents treat their children sets the stage for how their children are expected to treat others. If children see their parents treat others with kindness, caring, and concern, they learn to model these behaviors.

Providing children with a stable set of rules, along with clear consequences for breaking those rules, also helps foster moral development. At all ages, children respond best to specific, clearly defined rules and limits that are accompanied by an explanation of the reason behind them. For example, telling a five year old that she cannot watch a particular television show that many of her friends watch will have more impact if an explanation of your concerns about the content of the show is provided. This may not prevent her from continuing to nag about watching the show, but it will help her to understand that your rule is not based on the particular mood you're in that day!

The Golden Rule—"Do unto others as you would have them do unto you"—is another important basis for moral development. Although children at this age are not completely able to put themselves in another child's shoes, using recent memories and their imagination can help them to see how another child might feel. When your child tells you a story of a child at school calling another child names, use this situation to have your child "imagine" how each of those children might have felt.

Setting a positive example for your child can mean behaving in a particular way as well as discussing with (or, at least, in front of) her your own moral decisions and the reasons behind them. Pointing out moral behaviors in others is another way of providing positive examples to your child.

Establishing a strong moral foundation for your child helps her to deal with the confrontations she may encounter on the playground, in school, and at home. When a child has a good value system, she is better able to handle negative situations with others. In addition, early moral development gives children the strength to resist more powerful concerns, such as drugs, cheating, or stealing.

As parents, it is important to remember that you are talking to a five year old. Children this age are not able to attend to long, windy lectures about right and wrong. They forget easily. The discussion you had last night may be completely forgotten by the next day (or even the next hour). Keep your message clear, and let your child be an active participant in discussions of moral issues. Remember that many five year olds make a decision based on what benefits them the most. It is not until later years that children begin to express concern about what others will think of them and only in late adolescence and adulthood that there is an internalized sense of right and wrong.

Finally, it is important to monitor outside influences, such as television and peers. Television bombards children with the message that violent behavior, as well as alcohol and drug use, are acceptable behaviors. It is important to monitor the amount of television your child watches, as well as the type of program. Although peers are not as significant an influence at age five as they are in later years, they have a strong impact on what children view as right and wrong. Monitor your child's friendships, and if you have concerns, provide closer supervision and structure during playtime. Sometimes it is also possible to gently encourage friendships with children you feel may be a better influence on your child.

7

PERSONALITY DIFFERENCES

What is it that can make one child so gregarious, sociable, and outgoing and another child so painfully shy that he will not come out from behind his mother's leg to say hello to people he knows? If you were to observe a kindergarten class, you would probably be surprised by the extreme differences in the style of interactions among children. At one extreme are those children who are talkative with their peers, who volunteer for tasks, and who offer comments in a confident fashion. This is in sharp contrast to those children who tend to stay by themselves, who rarely interact with their peers, and who would like to hide under the table when the teacher asks for volunteers.

These differing personality styles are simply something with which children are born. Extroverts are those children who tend to draw energy from other people and things around them. They need the company of others and are constantly looking for friends to be around them. When they are alone, they become whiny or bored.

Parents of extroverts often have a house full of other children, just so their child will be content. Teachers may report problems these children have with chatting in class or difficulty keeping their hands off other children's belongings. It may be difficult for them to wait their turn to speak because they have an immediate answer for most questions. As soon as children arrive home from school, they seek immediate attention to recount all their experiences from the day.

Introverts, those children who need time alone to recharge, present a very different and often concerning picture to parents. These are the children who are very comfortable being alone. Sometimes they play with one or two others, but there is no urgency to have friends around. Many times, parents have to encourage their child to call another friend. These children are often described as slow to warm up, and they may withdraw from new situations or people. They may be more talkative at home than with strangers or at school, primarily because they are more comfortable at home.

These children learn best by reading and listening rather than participating in hands-on activities. They may demonstrate a strong sense of personal space and are protective of their possessions. Being forced to share is a frustrating situation for introverted children. When they arrive home from school, they need time to process their experiences from the day. They will probably be reluctant to talk about their day as soon as they arrive home and would rather spend time by themselves.

In school, these two personality types respond better to different approaches. For the outgoing, extroverted child, there is a need for lots of opportunities to talk. Space where they can work with friends is beneficial, as are periods during the day when they can be in physical contact with other children (circle time, recess, and gym time). Teachers can help the extrovert by speaking a child's name before asking a question. This helps your extroverted child learn to take turns.

In contrast, introverted children need a chance to watch and listen before participating in an activity. If they know what will be discussed ahead of time, they are more likely to participate in the discussion. They are comfortable with a quiet reading area away from other children and space where they can observe the ongoing activities. Unlike the outgoing child, an introverted child prefers circle time and other activities during which it's okay to sit apart from other children.

For the most part, the introverted child causes more concern that the extroverted child. They are frequently labeled "shy" and sometimes are judged to have social difficulties. Is it possible to help an introverted child become more outgoing?

To a certain extent, introverted children can become more comfortable in social situations. As parents, you can focus on opportunities to build self-confidence. Commend your child for attempting something that is difficult. Guiding your child into nonthreatening interactions can also help overcome social difficulties. Encouraging him to spend time with children who are not overbearing or intimidating will help him become more comfortable in social situations. When a new social situation comes up, try to introduce it on a gradual basis. Instead of accepting invitations to five birthday parties in a week, accept one invitation to a party that might not be too overwhelming (small number of children or a child with whom your child has had social contact).

Perhaps the most important factor to remember is to avoid labeling your child shy. Very often, parents can be heard telling other adults, "Don't mind him, he's just very shy." Comments like this, although not meant to hurt a child, can cause embarrassment and make a child acutely sensitive to the fact that social situations are difficult. Having it brought to the attention of others serves only to make the situation worse.

Comments from other adults about your child's "shyness" are best handled with a simple response: "He takes a little time to feel comfortable in new situations," or "He tends to be on the quiet side."

As with many of the other personality factors discussed in this section, if your child's shyness is having a significant impact on his ability to engage in day-to-day activities, it may be advisable to seek the help of a qualified professional. There are very specific programs available for children with social difficulties that focus on increasing the child's involvement in different social situations while decreasing the anxiety experienced.

8

FEARS

Bugs, monsters, ghosts, and noises in the basement are only a few of the many fears experienced by five-year-old children. Some children are more fearful than others, but for most, fears tend to focus on grotesque and spooky creatures. Children this age may also develop fears and anxieties about being lost, being alone or in the dark, accidents, and death.

Where do these fears come from? In some instances, they are brought on by some type of traumatic experience, real or not. An isolated dream about a monster may lead to fears about going to bed at night because monsters are in the closet or under the bed. A child who wanders away from Mom in the store may then develop ongoing anxieties about being lost or alone.

For other children, events that are beyond their comprehension may lead to fears and anxieties. News stories about children who are kidnapped or traumatic situations, such as an earthquake or a serious car accident, can cause a child to develop fears about being lost or anxieties about herself or others dying. As adults, we often become immune to the ongoing reports of disasters on television. When the TV is left on during dinnertime or while the children are playing in the same room, we need to be sensitive to the impact these reports may be having on the child who does not understand as well as we adults. Action movies and certain TV shows depicting dangerous sitiuations can also be a source of fears and anxiety in young children.

Finally, children are greatly influenced by the people around them. If friends, siblings, or even Mom and Dad express fears about different situations, a sensitive child may tune into these anxieties and begin to have the same concerns. A child who is sensitive and fearful by nature may not be able to determine that an adult is fooling when he says, "the bogeyman will get you!" For that particular child, such a statement may be very real and stir up all sorts of fears and anxieties.

Scary dreams or nightmares are quite common for children in this age group. They may occur on a more frequent basis if your child is ill or under some type of stress. Feelings of anxiety or guilt about having done something wrong can also bring on nightmares. For many children between the ages of five and six, it is very difficult to distinguish between what is a dream and what is reality.

What is the best way for you, as parents, to cope with your child's fears and anxieties? First, and most important, respect your child's fear. Putting a child down for being a "scaredy cat" only causes your child to feel shame and embarrassment. Try to be empathetic with your child's feelings with such statements as, "I know how frightened you must be" or "It's very scary to have those kinds of dreams." Such statements communicate respect for your child's feelings.

Be reassuring to your child by showing your love and protection. Let your child know you are there to protect her by providing a gentle hug or caress. Reassuring your child that you are in the next room or right upstairs at night helps her return to sleep after a nightmare. If your child wants to stay with you, it is better for you to stay in your child's room than to have her stay in your room.

Use fairy tales or fantasies to help a child reduce fears. Children who are able to identify with a hero or heroine in a story and tell how that person might handle the same fear can often use this way of coping in their own situation.

If a fear is truly interfering with your child's ability to go through her daily routine, helping her experience the fear in a safe, harmless way may be the necessary solution. For example, if your child has a strong fear of dogs, start by reading some books about dogs. Once your child is comfortable with that, move on to watching some movies about dogs. Along the way, point out that many dogs are gentle and tame. The next step may be to walk past a pet store, stopping to look in the window. Gradually increase your child's exposure to dogs in a very controlled way until she is ready to touch a real dog. This type of gradual exposure is useful for many fears. Some fears are so ingrained, however, that the help of a professional counselor may be warranted.

It is also important to realize that some fears are very rational and appropriate. A child who has been bitten by a dog will most likely be fearful of dogs.

Most fears diminish with age. If a fear doesn't diminish or if it interferes with your child's ability to complete everyday activities (the child who won't go to a friend's house because they have a dog), there is reason to be concerned and to seek outside help.

9

TEACHING YOUR CHILD ABOUT STRANGERS

With all the news reports about children being kidnapped from shopping malls, cars, and outside their homes, parents are now faced with the task of teaching their children about strangers. Inherent in this is maintaining the balance between teaching children to treat strangers with appropriate caution without having them lose the trust that comes with childhood.

For most preschoolers and five year olds, someone who acts nicely to them is thought of as being nice. In today's society, it is often difficult for us, as adults, to determine whether the friendly salesperson at our door is safe to talk to or not. Now we are faced with the task of teaching our children how to be cautious in the same situations.

It is helpful to incorporate rules for dealing with strangers into guidelines for personal safety. Along with the rules about crossing the street, walking home with a friend, or being in the house alone, add rules about talking to or taking things from strangers. These conversations with your child should have a calm and confident tone with an emphasis on the fact that dangerous individuals are the exception *not* the rule. Emphasizing to your child that it is better to be safe than sorry may help to eliminate frightening overtones.

When you are talking to your child about strangers, it is important to adjust your communication style to your child's temperament. If your child tends to be outgoing and sociable, you need to be clear and firm with your rules and guidelines. If, on the other hand, your child is shy and timid, you should use a more "matter-of-fact" approach to avoid frightening him.

Providing rules and guidelines that tell a child what he can do as opposed to what he shouldn't do is more helpful. Some specific rules follow:

- "You may go in a car with . . . ." Include people who may have to pick your child up from school in case of illness, relatives, and other people you would allow your child to be with.
- If you are lost, try to find a policeman. If you can't find a policeman, try to get help from someone working in a store or business.
- Don't answer the door if Mom or Dad is taking a shower or is outside.
- If someone stops in a car when you are walking by yourself, run to the nearest house (or store) and bang loudly on the door.
- If a stranger tries to walk away with you, yell loudly, "You are not my parent!"

Periodically, check your child's responses to different situations. Asking such questions as, "What would you do if someone stopped and offered you a ride?" or "What would you do if we were in a store and someone tried to walk away with you?" helps you to gain insight into how well your child has absorbed the rules about strangers.

Respecting your child's feelings will help him learn to trust his own judgment. When your child tells you he doesn't like Aunt Gertrude because she "kisses too much," avoid trying to convince him that she's a nice lady who is happy to see him.

Accepting his feelings about Aunt Gertrude and providing suggestions on how to deal with her overpowering behavior will help your child trust his feelings and opinions about all people, including strangers.

Finally, teach your child that his body belongs to himself. This is often an uncomfortable discussion for some parents to have with their child, but it is extremely important. Whatever terminology you choose to use with your child, the focus should be on the fact that no one except you, his parents, or a doctor should see or touch his body. Discuss the differences between appropriate touches and inappropriate touches. Reinforce with your child that he should tell you if *anyone* touches him in ways that make him feel uncomfortable.

If your child expresses the fact that he is uncomfortable with good old Aunt Gertrude hugging and kissing him, observe the interaction the next time she comes to visit. Tell Aunt Gertrude that your child feels uncomfortable, and help your child develop things he can say when Aunt Gertrude comes to visit. If the adult does not listen to your concerns or those voiced by your child, make sure that you are around when the visits take place. You may then need to step in and redirect the interaction if you see your child becoming uncomfortable.

With all children, patience and sensitivity are the keys to helping them incorporate these important messages into their daily routines. For parents, it is important to maintain a calm, secure approach in the hope that your child will keep that balance between cautiousness with strangers and the trusting nature of childhood.

10

DEALING WITH ANGER AND AGGRESSION

D ealing with your child's anger can be confusing and distressing. It is often difficult to handle anger in children because of the feelings it can stir up in us as adults. Anger is a temporary emotional state often caused by frustration. When children are unable to get what they want, the emotional response may be an angry outburst.

Anger may also be related to a number of other factors, including anxiety and low self-esteem or a way of avoiding painful feelings. Children who feel anxious because they have no control over a situation may express their anxiety as anger. Because young children have difficulty labeling many emotions, disappointment and sometimes even sadness may be communicated as anger.

Aggression is often related to underlying feelings of anger but is defined as behaviors that are intended to hurt someone, either physically or emotionally. Teasing, physical attacks, and destructiveness are some of the ways aggression is shown. Many aggressive children are likely to suffer rejection by their peers, which keeps the cycle growing.

Culture, upbringing, and the degree of exposure each person has had to aggression play a role in what is defined as aggressive behavior. You may intervene quickly if your child engages in a pushing and shoving match with another child, whereas the other parent may think that kind of behavior is acceptable from children.

How do children learn aggressive behavior? Modeling and reinforcement of certain behaviors can result in an increase in aggression. If a child is given attention and praise for being aggressive in sports, that behavior will most likely become a part of that child's repertoire. If parents use physical punishment (hitting) when their child hits someone, they are modeling aggressive behavior. Additionally, it is almost impossible to find television shows today that do not depict aggressive behavior in one form or another.

Children who behave aggressively may also be seeking attention. If Mom or Dad comes running every time Susie pushes her baby brother down, this may be the key to her behavior. Remember that attention does not have to be positive for it to be desirable to a young child. Negative attention is better than no attention at all!

The key to dealing with aggressive behavior is trying to understand the underlying cause. Aggressive behavior should not be ignored or tolerated, nor should parents overreact to aggressive behaviors. If the underlying cause is a plea for attention, try to provide that attention for positive, appropriate behaviors. Tell your child what behaviors please you by using "I" statements: I like the way you helped your baby sister today. I really appreciate it when you play quietly while I'm on the telephone. I think it's great that you were willing to share your favorite toy with your friend.

Children who act aggressively toward others should be penalized with an appropriate consequence. Hitting or strong verbal punishments serve only to reinforce the same behavior you are trying to eliminate.

Help your child to understand how the other person feels. At five years of age, children are not fully able to put themselves in another's shoes. Encourage your child to talk about her own feelings. Let her know that angry feelings are natural and acceptable, but hitting and saying mean things to another child are not. If necessary, provide suggestions for using words to express angry feelings. Instead of grabbing toys from other children, encourage your child to say, "May I have a turn with that toy now?"

Throughout this book one concept keeps coming to the forefront: modeling appropriate behavior. If we, as parents or other significant adults, are unable to express anger in appropriate ways, how can we expect our children to learn to express their feelings in ways that are constructive and healthy?

11

THE SENSITIVE CHILD

From the child who bursts into tears at the mildest reprimand to the child who is fearful of making even the slightest mistake, there is evidence suggesting that these traits are biologically based rather than learned. Is there any way to make these children tougher, to get them to deal more effectively with criticism? The answer seems to be yes and no. Although it is not possible to make drastic changes in a child's personality characteristics, it is possible to help him learn to control the degree to which he reacts to things.

Taking risks and failing is an important part of life. When children become so focused on the possibility of failure and, with it, the criticism of others, they avoid taking risks. This is sometimes seen in negative behaviors, such as refusing to do schoolwork, or in accepting negative consequences rather than face a task that seems too difficult. Children who try too hard for fear of making a mistake may develop nervous habits, have trouble falling asleep, or have nightmares. For young children, this is a crucial time because they are just beginning to develop a sense of how smart they are.

What are the steps to making a sensitive child a little tougher? First, boost self-esteem by focusing on positive behaviors and capabilities. Provide praise for accomplishments. Some parents don't realize the message they are giving their child with such statements as, "That was great, but you can do better next time." The sensitive child may not hear the first part of this statement and may focus only on the fact that his performance was not good enough.

Encourage your child's attempts at new tasks. When your child wants to try something new or something that has proved to be difficult for him in the past, avoid saying, "It's too hard for you." If you believe the task may be too difficult, work alongside your child, modeling the appropriate behavior. Provide direction and suggestions when necessary but try not to take over when you see your child start to struggle.

Ask your child to help around the house. Many times, a child who is overly sensitive and unsure of himself will not volunteer to do things for fear of failing. By choosing a task for him, you can encourage your child to become actively involved and less fearful of taking a risk.

Talk about your own mistakes with your child. Admit errors, and discuss possible solutions. When you ask your child to talk about his mistakes, focus on feelings by asking such questions as, "How did it feel?" Empathize with your child's feelings before asking how he would correct the problem or mistake. Condition your child to take criticism by softening it with affection. A discussion of a problem behavior may be more acceptable for your sensitive five year old when he's sitting on your lap getting a hug as opposed to sitting on a hard chair receiving a lecture.

Don't reward supersensitive reactions. Young children can quickly learn that crying and pouting will gain attention from Mom or Dad. Although it is difficult for parents to watch their child in a painful situation, rewarding these reactions serves only to make the situation worse.

Remember that encouragement is the key to developing confidence, competency, and self-respect. At the same time, however, it is important to keep in mind that not all children will be dynamic, confident risk takers. Sometimes we need to take a step back and look at the expectations we have for our children. By providing your child with a supportive, loving learning environment you will help him to reach his potential. Try to keep your focus on what your child is able to do rather than on things that may prove difficult for him.

12

DEALING WITH FRUSTRATION

Almost any time young children are faced with a big "No" to their requests, desires, and wishes, frustration results. For most parents, dealing with a child's frustration is itself a frustrating event. Your child can't have what she wants—a piece of candy or a new toy—and you can't have what you want—a cooperative, pleasant child.

Children are not born able to tolerate frustration. As with many other skills, learning to tolerate frustration is a developmental process. Hunger, tiredness, and illness all serve to lower your child's frustration tolerance.

Children also attempt to accomplish tasks that are beyond their means. This is the way children learn, and the frustration that accompanies it is both healthy and necessary for learning.

Frustration also results when children don't get what they want. This may be the result of limit setting by parents (no candy before dinner) or events out of their control (toy doesn't work or Mom gets sick on the day of the circus).

How do you help your child (and yourself) get through these frustrating times? When your child is not feeling stressed, teach patience by helping him to delay gratification. When he asks you to play a game while you're in the middle of a task, have him wait for a short period of time. Praise him for being patient, and gradually work on increasing the time he has to wait.

Empathize with your child's feelings of frustration. Such statements as, "You worked so hard on that building and it keeps falling over," validates his feelings. Verbalizing the problem can also help pull for possible solutions. After empathizing about the building, saying something like "How can you make it stronger so that it will stay up?" gives your child a cue about solving the problem.

Provide an alternative for your child when he can't have a desired object. When your child asks for candy in the grocery store, suggest another, more acceptable alternative. This may not always work, especially for the child who is intent on a candy bar. For other children, however, the alternative choice may be reasonable. If your child is engaged in an activity that is causing frustration, suggest that he walk away for a few minutes or try to engage him in a different activity for a period of time.

Some typical situations that cause frustration for five year olds include wanting anything and everything when shopping, sharing with friends and siblings, asserting their independence with dressing, dealing with household rules, such as bedtime, dealing with losing, and making mistakes.

Sometimes it is helpful to address a problem before it occurs. You know your child better than anyone else and can probably predict the type of reaction he may have to particular situations. If your child has difficulty in a store, explain ahead of time that you are not buying any toys or candy today. Similarly, if household rules are a source of frustration, give a warning to allow your child to prepare. Letting him know there are 15 minutes until bedtime or dinner may help alleviate some of the frustration felt when it's time to turn off the television or put away the toys. For the child who has difficulty sharing toys, scheduling play dates for a limited period of time (perhaps start with 30 minutes) may help build in success. As your child is able to share for longer periods without reaching his frustration level, you can begin to increase play time.

Providing a positive consequence for appropriate behavior will also help your child learn to deal better with frustration. When you go into a store and your child allows you to shop without asking for every toy or candy he sees, a small treat along with positive feedback will reinforce the appropriate behavior. Be specific in your statement so your child knows exactly what behavior is being praised. "I'm proud of you for not asking for anything today. It makes shopping much more pleasant." You can use similar statements for other situations that may be a source of frustration for your child. Small treats can consist of a variety of things including candy, a quick trip to the playground, or an extra story for being ready for bed without a fuss.

When your child misbehaves out of frustration, it is important to provide firm consequences. If your child experiences frustration during an activity that is so intense he gives up, intervene as quickly as possible so that he has an opportunity to experience success. Modeling patience for your child in day-to-day routines is an important component in his ability to learn to deal with his own frustrations.

13

YOUR CHILD CAN HAVE MANNERS

Y ou can't make me! You're not the boss! Such comments may be your five year old's expression of independence. They are considered by most people to be rude and fresh, however.

Politeness is the ability to show basic respect for the feelings of others. When children start to talk, there is a tendency to pick up on the language of others. Even on a very young level, it is not unusual to have a child come home from nursery school or day care and repeat some of the unpleasant comments heard from other children!

By the time children reach the age of five, they are old enough to say please, thank you, and excuse me. Greeting people, both in person and on the telephone, is a reasonable skill to expect from your child. Interruptions while you are talking to someone should be minimal at this point. Most five year olds should be able to wait in a restaurant or store without excessive fidgeting. Manners at the dinner table should be well developed by this time. This means using utensils and a napkin properly with minimal reminders. As your child begins to learn to print her name, signing (and, for some children, writing) thank-you cards can be expected.

How do you get your child to accomplish these tasks? Being a positive role model for your child is the first step. Most of us tend to speak politely to other adults, but we sometimes

40

forget when we are talking to our own children. Remembering to add "please" when asking your child to do something can go a long way. Reinforce good manners when you hear them. Telling your child "I really like the way you said thank you to Mrs. Jones" increases the chances that the behavior will occur again.

By age five, most children can understand the consequences of making rude remarks to others. Depending on the situation and the degree of rudeness, reprimanding your child and asking for an apology is a reasonable way to handle the situation. In other situations, it may be better to agree on a code word that you can use to avoid embarrassment. This may be helpful when your child is showing off in front of her friends or testing the limits.

If your child does not respond to your verbal reprimands or code words, you may need to role play how to be polite. Use a specific situation as an example, and ask your child to think of different things she could say. For example, if your child has difficulty politely asking for something, practice having her ask several different people—you, her grandparents, a friend's mother, and a teacher. It may be helpful for you to begin by playing the part of your child so you can provide a model for appropriate behavior. Then have your child play herself, and rehearse these responses in a nonthreatening situation.

Instead of giving your child a direct command about manners (Stop slouching in your chair), give her a reminder about the rule (Remember, we sit up straight at the table). If your child is in a situation she doesn't always handle well, give her a gentle prompt. When someone in the store hands her something, help her find the correct response by saying, "You know the right thing to say."

Sometimes we find ourselves using too many words to correct behaviors. If this is the case, use nonverbal reminders

41

to improve manners. Instead of responding verbally to such statements as, "More milk," hold the milk out of reach to remind your child she forgot to say "please."

When rudeness seems to be related to your child's "declaration of independence," restate those feelings and provide an example of how you would like your child to respond. Validate your child's feeling with a statement like, "I know you don't like me telling you what to do, but you may not be rude to me." Continue by providing an example of an appropriate way to express feelings.

When you feel there is no hope for having a polite child, remember that this is another example of behaviors that can be modified. Talking to your child with respect is the most beneficial way to help her act politely. If your tone of voice is harsh and demanding, your child will model the same behavior when she is speaking to you and others. Sometimes children use polite words, but their tone of voice can quickly eliminate any polite message.

Focusing on politeness and manners is not always easy when the demands of parenthood start to take their toll, but reminding yourself of the long-term consequences may make it easier!

14

~~~~~~

THE "DIFFICULT" CHILD

A ll children are born with a certain style of responding, or *temperament*. Most children's temperament fits well with the environment around them. For others, however, temperamental characteristics interfere with their ability to adapt easily to their everyday world.

Nine temperamental characteristics, or *traits*, were originally identified in 1956 by a group of researchers who studied individuals from infancy to adulthood. These characteristics included activity level, distractibility, intensity, regularity, negative persistence, sensory threshold, approach and withdrawal, adaptability, and mood. These temperamental qualities have a range and, when assembled in a package, can make up a "difficult" child. Children who exhibit these qualities are quite normal but can also be quite overwhelming for parents who attempt to have their child fit with the rest of the family.

Such behaviors as having difficulty with transitions, being easily upset, expressing discomfort with and rejection of new clothing, displaying irregular eating and sleeping patterns, and a high activity level are some of the things that confuse parents. As parents attempt to cope with these behaviors using typical behavior management skills, the results are ineffective, and power struggles emerge. When children reach the age of five and become more self-sufficient in their skills, these struggles may focus on attending skills, impulsiveness, sharing, and clothing.

The best way to determine whether the behaviors you are trying to cope with are caused by temperament is by assessing whether these characteristics have been present since birth. Difficult children are often described as having been irritable or colicky as infants. Irregular sleeping and eating patterns were often present, as were high-intensity behaviors, such as screaming. If, on the other hand, these behaviors emerged recently and you can connect them to a specific event, such as family stress, a new school, or a new sibling, they are not a result of temperament.

If your usual behavior management techniques don't work, what is the answer to coping with a difficult child's behavior? Dr. Stanley Tureki, author of *The Difficult Child* and founder of the Difficult Child Program in New York, suggests a five-step program for dealing with the difficult child: 1. Evaluate your child's behaviors, your responses, and the family reactions to determine which behaviors are the most important to change. 2. Regain adult authority through discipline that works. 3. Use effective management techniques. 4. Seek family guidance if necessary. 5. Establish support groups for other parents. *The Difficult Child* is strongly recommended as a resource for those parents who believe they may have a difficult child.

The first step in handling any type of behavior problem is to assess your ability to intervene at that time. If you need to go to the store but you have a headache and are in a rotten mood, engaging in a battle to have your child leave his favorite television show may not be the best thing to do.

Second, remember that you are the adult and try to not get hooked into your child's behavior. Attempt to maintain a neutral attitude: do not respond emotionally. Focusing on the behavior, not the motives behind the behavior, helps you deal more effectively.

Determine whether the behavior needs intervention. If your child is being somewhat noisy but is not causing harm to anyone (except for intensifying your headache!), it may be more effective to get two aspirin and take refuge in another room than to try to intervene.

The next few keys discuss in more detail some effective behavior management techniques to use with your child. It is important to try to differentiate those behaviors that are the result of your child's temperament and those over which he truly has control. Your decision to intervene and the method of intervention may be different for both.

15

TALKING TO YOUR
FIVE YEAR OLD

E stablishing a good basis of communication with your five-year-old child is a skill that will help you well into your child's adolescence. If you stop and listen to your friends, relatives, or even strangers talking to their children, you may be surprised at the different styles of communication you hear. This key focuses on how to talk to children when you are helping them deal with their feelings, when you are attempting to have them cooperate with you, and when you are trying to encourage independence. The focus is on how to listen effectively and how to minimize the amount of language used to get your point across.

All of us want to know that we are being heard when we talk to someone, especially when we are upset. Busy schedules, stress, telephones ringing, or two other people asking questions at the same time often make it difficult to give your full attention when your child is trying to talk to you. As impossible as it may seem, it is extremely important to listen attentively. Put down the newspaper, let the telephone ring, or ask the other children to wait for five minutes while you listen to what your child is saying.

When your child relates something to you, acknowledge her feelings. Children don't want to hear that they are too sensitive or overreacting to something that may be very upsetting to them. A simple nod of your head or "I understand" is all that may be needed to let your child know you acknowledge her feelings. Help your child identify the feelings by giving them names. "It sounds as if you were pretty angry" or "You really liked that doll a lot" lets your child know that you are listening and accepting her feelings.

There are many times when you can listen to feelings but are unable to solve your child's problem. You can give your child a wish in fantasy, however. If your child is upset because she did not get the toy she asked for on her birthday, a statement like, "I wish I could change this toy into the one you really wanted," can sometimes help to ease her upset.

How many times have you heard an adult, frustrated in an attempt to engage a child's cooperation, say something like the following? "How many times have I told you to pick up your toys? We go through the same thing every day. You pull out all your toys and then you refuse to pick them up! All I do is talk to you. Why can't you just do it the first time I ask you?" And on, and on, and on. Most children will have stopped listening after the first sentence, especially if this is the usual way of handling noncompliance.

To engage a child's cooperation, eliminate the unnecessary talking.

- Describe the problem in simple terms. "Your toys are all over the floor."
- Give your child information about the problem. "It would be helpful if your toys were picked up before we eat dinner."
- Instead of talking in paragraphs about the problem, use one word: "Susie, *toys!*"
- As your child starts to read, use notes to relay messages. A note reading "Put toys away" left on the toy box may help remind your child of what she is supposed to do.

Helping your five year old to become independent can be a dilemma for most parents. You don't want your child to make mistakes and suffer from failure, yet you know that children must undertake difficult tasks at which they may fail if they are to become responsible, independent human beings. There are some simple ways to foster independence, even with young children.

Allow them to make choices about the color of pants they want to wear, the breakfast cereal they want to eat, or the book they want to read. These choices should not be open ended but should consist of a forced choice between two alternatives you have picked out. "Do you want to wear your blue pants or your green pants today?"

When your child is struggling with a difficult task, instead of jumping in and completing it for her, offer some useful information. For example, if your child is having difficulty zippering her coat, help with a statement like, "Zippers can be hard to close. Sometimes if you hold onto the bottom of your coat the zipper may be easier to pull up."

When your child asks a question, don't be too quick to provide an answer. Turn the question back to your child to have her think more about the answer. There is always time to supply the correct answer later, after she has gone through the process of searching for the answer herself.

Encourage your child to use sources within the community when she has a specific question or wants to obtain more information. The librarian, a teacher, a school nurse, and a dentist are a few of the many people to whom your child can turn for help. Depending on the situation, these people may also be more powerful sources of information than Mom or Dad.

Taking some time to listen to the way you talk to your children can provide a wealth of information. The phrases we use, the degree to which we listen, and the amount of language we use can be changed to improve communication skills with children. These changes can often be all that is needed to eliminate other behavior issues that seem so overwhelming.

16

HELPING YOUR CHILD TO BEHAVE

Discipline does not mean the use of punishment to modify behavior. Effective discipline provides guidance and limits that help children grow into well-functioning individuals.

When children are first born, they are helpless individuals. Through the guidance and teaching of their parents they learn to clap hands, wave good-bye, play peek-a-boo, and numerous other skills. Discipline can and should be approached in the same way. This key discusses some of the many techniques for effective discipline. Whatever technique you use, consistency is the key. Many times parents try one technique for a few days, see no change in behavior, and quickly switch to something else. Choose one or two techniques that you will be able to use on a consistent basis, and give them time to have an effect. Remember, in some cases you may be trying to modify a behavior that has developed over five years!

Setting Limits

Children need the security of limits, of knowing what they can and cannot do. Limits help children know what to expect in a particular situation and provide guidelines for their behavior.

When you set limits for your child, it is important to make them short and clear. Long-winded descriptions of the rules has little impact on your child. Such statements as, "You may not climb on the furniture because you could fall" or "You may only cross the street with an adult (or older sibling) because you could get hit by a car," are some examples of short, concise rules.

Explain the reason for the rule or limit to your child. No one likes to be told what to do, even five year olds. If you can provide a simple explanation, there is more of a chance that your child will comply with the rule.

Whenever possible, remind your child of the rules before you have to enforce them. If, for example, your child has difficulty remembering to stop at the corner when bike riding, provide a simple reminder, such as, "Remember, you must stop at the corner and watch for cars" just before you and your child go out for a ride.

Be Positive

The first place to start an effective discipline program is with the positive. Praise is a very powerful and effective way to change behaviors. The tendency for most of us is to focus on the negative behaviors. Unfortunately, it is far more likely that we intervene when there is screaming, crying, or carrying on than there is when our children are quietly playing in the other room. It is possible, however, to retrain yourself to focus on the positive aspects of your child's behavior.

Identify, as clearly as possible, the behaviors you want to increase. Take the time to notice and mention when your child is engaged in these behaviors. For example, if Johnny has difficulty sharing with his younger sister, shift your focus to the one or two times you can catch him sharing well. Sometimes you must search and pay close attention, but eventually the proper behavior will occur!

Praise the behavior with such statements as, "I really like the way you are sharing your toys with your sister!" It is very important to point out to children the specific behavior rather than praise the child for "being good." Don't be discouraged if the behavior doesn't occur too frequently at first. Take any opportunity you can find, even the times when sharing was actually giving away the piece of candy he didn't like! Using charts to monitor the occurrence of positive behaviors is also useful. This is discussed in more detail in the next key.

Decreasing Behaviors

Praise can also be useful when you are trying to decrease a negative behavior. Praising your child for *not* engaging in a negative behavior helps to decrease its occurrence. If your child typically whines when he asks for something, praise each time he asks without whining. "I really like the way you asked without whining." "Thank you for asking like a big kid." It may take awhile before you see the negative behaviors start to decrease, but eventually it will happen!

Providing Consequences

When you establish rules and limits with your child, it is also helpful to establish consequences to go along with not following those rules. *Natural consequences* are things that automatically occur in response to a behavior. If adults do not go to work, they do not get a paycheck. If you do not do the laundry, eventually you run out of clothing. Sometimes it is easy to overlook the natural consequences of behaviors for children. If your child refuses to eat dinner, the natural consequence is hunger. If he is mean to his friends, he will not have anyone to play with. When it is appropriate, allow your child to experience these natural consequences.

Other behaviors can be followed by logical consequences that you, the parent, impose. If your child misuses a toy, the toy is removed. If something is damaged, have your child play a role in repairing the damage. If your child makes a mess with paints or crayons, have him help clean up. Logical consequences establish a clear link between the behavior and the outcome.

Time-Out

There may be times when you must use some type of negative intervention to modify behavior. Time-out is a very effective method for helping your child to regain control. For it to work however, time-out must be used properly.

Identify a place in your home to use for time-out. This might be your child's room, a chair in another part of the house, or some other, out of the way area.

Identify one or two behaviors that warrant the use of time-out, such as hitting, kicking, or talking back to an adult. Try to avoid using time-out for too many behaviors or behaviors that occur frequently. If you use time-out too much, it loses its effectiveness.

When your child is engaged in the targeted behavior you are trying to reduce, give one warning. (Physically hurting someone should be an automatic time-out. Don't give a warning.) If the behavior continues, tell your child he needs to take a five-minute time-out. The general recommendation for time-out is one minute per year of age (a three year old would have a three-minute time-out). Do not engage in any more verbalizations with your child, and if necessary, escort him to the time-out area.

Use a kitchen timer or the timer on your oven or microwave to monitor the time. If your child calls to you, do not respond verbally. If he attempts to leave the time-out area, escort him back with a simple statement, "The timer has not gone off yet." If the timer goes off and your child is still upset, a simple statement indicating that he can come out when he is calm should be sufficient.

Once the time-out is over, you may want to review the behavior briefly and why it is unacceptable. This should be the end of your interactions regarding a specific behavior. The slate is wiped clean, and you each go about your business.

Time-out can also be used in other places, such as other people's homes, stores (find an empty corner), or even your car, if necessary.

Removing Privileges

There may be times when you choose to take away a privilege as a consequence for breaking a rule. Removing a special television show, toys, or Nintendo can be effective if used properly. Removing TV on a night when nothing is on won't work! Taking away all your child's toys as a consequence for breaking one will probably worsen the situation, especially because he now has nothing to do except get into more trouble! Losing Nintendo for one day is more effective than losing it for one week. After a couple of days neither you nor your child will probably remember why the Nintendo was taken away in the first place!

Whatever the technique you use, remember these guidelines:

- Be consistent.
- Provide the consequence immediately after the behavior. If you wait too long, the connection between behavior and consequence is lost.
- Make sure the rewards or punishments are things your child cares about.
- Give it time to work! Miracles and behavior changes don't happen over night.

17

USING CHARTS TO
INCREASE
BEHAVIORS

A nother way to increase behaviors is with use of charts. Many children respond well because charts give them a way of visually monitoring both their behavior and the positive consequences of that behavior. Children can be active participants in developing a chart, maintaining it, and monitoring reinforcers.

There are several different ways to design a chart. It can be something as simple as putting a star or a happy face on a calendar for each day your child picks up her toys or gets herself dressed before the bus is waiting at the door. Other charts can be more elaborate, listing two to four different behaviors. Table 17.1 is an example of a simple chart.

The days of the week are listed down the side and the specific behaviors across the top. It is helpful to have your child participate in choosing the behaviors that will go on the chart. This gives you a chance to discuss why these behaviors are important. Also, having your child participate in making the chart gives her a sense of ownership. You can have your child draw or cut out a picture from magazines to depict the behavior being charted. Again, this makes it easier for her to know what behaviors are being charted as well as make her an active participant.

Table 17.1
A TYPICAL CHART FOR INCREASING BEHAVIORS

	Brush Teeth	*Get Dressed*	*Breakfast*
Sunday			
Monday			
Tuesday			
Wednesday			
Thursday			
Friday			
Saturday			

Behaviors on the chart should be described in positive terms, keeping in mind that these are behaviors you are trying to increase. If getting ready for school is difficult for your child, you can break down the behaviors needed to reach the final goal of being ready for the school bus. Include such behaviors as brush teeth, wash face, get dressed, eat breakfast, and pack school bag. Similarly, if getting ready for bed is a time of conflict for you and your child, you can include such behaviors as put toys away, put on pajamas, brush teeth, and wash face.

Each time you observe one of the behaviors, place some type of mark in the appropriate box—hash marks, stickers, stars, happy faces, or whatever your child likes. Allowing your child to place the sticker or mark on the chart also helps to increase her participation. Always pair the sticker or mark with verbal praise for the specific behavior.

Decide on several rewards that will be available for each day and the number of stars or marks needed to earn the reward. Daily rewards should consist of things that don't cost money. A special dessert, staying up 15 minutes later, and special time alone with Mom or Dad are some suggestions. You can set up a "menu," with your child listing the number of stars needed for each reward. For example, if you have four behaviors or tasks on the chart, your child may need to complete two for a special dessert, three for a special book, and all four to stay up 15 minutes later.

A more substantial reward can be used for the end of the week. Again, determine the number of stars needed, and set up a reward menu. You might include a video rental, playtime with a special friend, a small toy, lunch at McDonald's, or a trip to the park.

One major benefit of using a chart is that you can modify the number of stars needed for a reward as the frequency of the behavior increases. For example, if you decide your child needs to start picking up her toys (something she does only once or twice a week), she could earn a daily reward when she completes the task and, initially, a weekly reward if the toys are picked up two times during week. As the behavior occurs more frequently, you would increase the number of stars needed for her to earn the reward. Eventually, you can eliminate the daily rewards and use only the weekly rewards.

When using charts, keep in mind the following:

- Make sure your child is interested in the rewards you have chosen.
- Make the rewards attainable. If you are trying to increase a behavior that occurs only once or twice a week, don't set a goal of five or six stars. Even though your child gets a daily reward when the behavior occurs, she may never attain the weekly goal. This can be very discouraging for both you and your child and defeats the purpose of the chart.

- Start out small. Don't begin a chart with five or six behaviors. This is too overwhelming for both you and your child. You can always add (and delete) behaviors to the chart as changes occur.
- As the behaviors start to increase in frequency, increase the number of stars or marks needed to obtain a reward. The goal of a chart system is to increase the behavior to the point at which it is maintained by praise alone.

18

ADJUSTING TO A
WORKING MOM

It would be wonderful if our family situations were able to remain consistent and stable, with one parent going to work and the other staying home to take care of the children. Grandma and Grandpa live nearby and have frequent contact with their grandchildren. Unfortunately, this stability is far from commonplace in today's society.

Many mothers return to the workforce for financial reasons. When possible, many mothers can coordinate their return to work with their child's entrance into school. Although this often works well in minimizing the need for child care, it can still be difficult for a young child who has a strong attachment to his mother.

What is the best way to help your child cope with your return to work? First, consistent child care is extremely important. Your child will have less difficulty if he has the same child care routine every day. If possible, using a family member or person in your immediate neighborhood is ideal. If you need to use a day care setting or person with whom your child has not had previous contact, try to arrange to visit with your child before you leave him by himself.

Maintain a routine during the week so your child knows what to expect. Trying to get children out to school and yourself out to work is a chaotic undertaking. Preparing lunches the night before, picking out clothes, or choosing items for show-

and-tell ahead of time helps to eliminate some of the confusion. Similarly, a set routine for the evening when you get home also helps your child to cope better. This does not mean that you must set up a schedule that is so rigid there can be no modifications. Flexibility is the key when you are a working mother.

Prepare yourself for your child's reaction to your return to work. If you have been able to stay at home and care for your child on a daily basis, you may feel a certain amount of anger and resentment from your child when you go back to work. All of a sudden, your child must adjust to a new person's rules and regulations. At the same time, he is without all the special things only a mother can provide. When you are anxious to get home in the evening to see your child, you may be met by someone who is angry or confused, who feels he was deserted. How your child experiences your absence during the day may be very different from the way you experience your child's absence. Try not to react if you are faced with this anger when you get home. Try to verbalize for your child what he may be feeling, and explain how difficult it is for you to leave him as well.

To reduce some of the stress that comes with returning to work, try to simplify your life. Don't put yourself into a frenzy by trying to prepare a gourmet meal every night or insisting that your child have a bath each and every evening. It is far more important to spend some "quality" time with your child doing something that you both enjoy than it is to worry about how many vegetables he is eating!

Make use of the technology that is available to eliminate some of the confusion when you get home. A telephone answering machine to respond to phone calls while you are preparing dinner or a microwave oven to make a quick meal can help your balancing act. These helpers may also give you additional time to spend with your child. Allow your child to watch television for the short time you are preparing dinner. This limits the distractions and interruptions that may lengthen your time in the kitchen.

It is important to remember that the whole process of returning to work—establishing a routine, adjusting to the separation, and maintaining your sanity—gets easier with time. Keeping your flexibility and a sense of humor are the keys to making your transition back to work a little easier.

19

RAISING A RESPONSIBLE CHILD

When children reach late childhood to early adolescence, there is an almost automatic expectation that they will show signs of responsibility. Many parents are at a loss when that responsibility is not forthcoming. Yet, for many families, attempts were not made to teach their children to be responsible for themselves, their belongings, and as members of the family system at an early age.

Children, even at a very young age, are capable of developing responsibilities. This does not take away their childhood or put parents in the category of slave drivers. What it does, however, is encourage self-direction and decision making. In taking responsibility, first for herself and then as a member of the family, a child is able to experience a sense of accomplishment and satisfaction. These early responsibilities also lead to later responsibility as a member of a larger community and society.

How, as parents, can you begin to teach your child responsibility? First, the earlier children begin to assume family-related responsibilites, the more likely they will accept them as a part of their daily routine. Tasks should be geared to the child's age and ability level. Very young children can learn to be responsible for picking up their toys and keeping their rooms neat. As they get older, children can assist with such chores as sorting laundry, putting it away, setting the table, or putting groceries away. Some children might be able to make their own grocery list or help with cooking. Five-year-old children are also capable of helping in the yard by picking up leaves or watering plants.

It is important to allow your child to have a say in the decision-making process when you are trying to identify specific chores and tasks. Each of us likes to have some sense of control, and you are more likely to get compliance if your child is given a choice of the tasks for which she is responsible. It is also extremely important to be consistent once responsibilties are identified. We live in a very busy society and are often engaged in a large number of activities. Sometimes it is far more easy to complete a task ourselves than it is to remind our children four or five times. The question is, which is more beneficial? In the long run, we would all probably agree that it is more beneficial for our children to have the ongoing responsibility than it is to do it ourselves. This may necessitate consequences for not completing tasks. Loss of a special dessert or 15 minutes of television time are some suggestions. Making special privileges contingent on completing tasks is also useful. The Saturday rule may be that no one is allowed to go out to play until all chores are done.

In addition to identifying specific tasks for your child to complete, it is also important to make her responsible for correcting her own mistakes. For example, if something was spilled, have her play a part in cleaning it up. If she broke something, she should be made responsible for attempting to repair it. Keeping in mind your child's age, this may mean having her provide some help while you do most of the work. This still gives her a sense of responsibility and ownership.

When children are given responsibility at an early age, they begin to feel as if they are making a real and important contribution to the family. Making your child responsible is not intended to be a burden on him or on you as parents. It is important for children to know their capabilities and be able to act upon them. Remember the long-term goal: helping your child to become an independent and self-sufficient individual. As you see your child become more confident in her abilities, you will become more confident that you are on the right track.

20

IMPROVING YOUR CHILD'S SELF-ESTEEM

The words get tossed around in child development literature, and even nonscientists may talk about those people who have "poor self-esteem." What is self-esteem, and where does it come from? *Self-esteem* is, in basic terms, a person's pride in himself. To have self-esteem, we must feel both lovable and capable as a person. This takes us back to family, teachers, and early caregivers, all of whom serve to establish a basic sense of security for young children. The verbal environment in which a child is raised plays an extremely valuable role in the development of self-esteem. How much adults say to a child, what they say, how they speak, and how well they listen all contribute to that basic sense of security and love (or lack of it).

A positive verbal environment is one in which words are used to show affection and interest in a child. When adults listen attentively, speak courteously, and use a child's interest as the basis for conversation, they are telling the child they are interested in him. This type of positive verbal atmosphere increases the likelihood that children view adults as a source of comfort and support.

There are literally hundreds of ways that we, as parents, can foster our child's self-esteem. First, and most important, is providing unconditional love. The message that no matter what you do or how you behave you will always be loved must be relayed to children on a daily basis. This is the true basis of security. When you get angry with your child (and you will!), express your anger by using "I" messages. There is a big difference between statements like, "I get really upset and angry when you are not careful and spill your milk" and "What is wrong with you? Can't you ever do anything right? Don't you have a brain in your head?" No one would feel very good after a statement like this!

Learn to listen to your child. Chatty five year olds tend to go on and on about things that may not seem as important as the television or newspaper. Children need your full attention when they speak, or they need to be told that you will be able to give them your full attention in five minutes. This lets them know you are interested in what they have to say.

Take your child's feelings seriously. What we may view as unimportant can be earth shattering to a five year old. Find something to appreciate about your child everyday. There are days that may seem like a difficult task, but have confidence that you can find something!

Show your child respect—for his possessions, opinions, and choices. When adults question a child's decision about something or demean a choice he has made, they undermine his pride in himself. Children at age five are beginning to self-evaluate. Their sense of confidence is far from strong and can be easily destroyed by negative comments.

If your child puts himself down, it is important to intervene immediately. Help to counter his put-downs by teaching him to focus on his abilities. Share your own feelings about yourself and about things you may have felt at that age. Help your child to focus on his uniqueness, and express your love nonverbally with hugs and embraces.

As a parent, it is extremely important to avoid giving your child mixed messages. Be clear about the rules and requests you make of your child. If you make a promise, keep it. If you can't keep it, explain to your child why and make an extra effort not to make promises you can't keep. Model appropriate behavior for your child. You are probably the most important person in your child's life, and what he sees from you will be incorporated into his feelings about himself.

21

~~~~~~

HELPING YOUR CHILD UNDERSTAND PREJUDICE

We live in a diverse society with people from different religions, races, political beliefs, and nationalities. Unfortunately, many stereotypes are associated with this diversity, which often lead to discrimination and prejudice. It is not uncommon to hear jokes that focus on a specific characteristic or a certain ethnic group. The attitudes and opinions that are formed about people simply because they belong to a specific race, religion, or nationality are the basis of prejudice. When people act on the basis of prejudices and stereotypes, they are engaging in discrimination.

Even in the most progressive, liberal areas, children are exposed to the stereotypes and prejudices of those around them. Whether it is someone telling a joke about a particular nationality or someone making a comment about a group of people based on their religion, it is difficult to protect children from these attitudes. Sometimes even our own family members hold specific attitudes that, in one way or another, are expressed to children. Other children can also communicate these attitudes during play or, more dramatically, in their unwillingness to play with certain children. Children who have a poor self-image tend to be more likely to develop prejudices. For those children, putting down another person makes them feel more important.

As a parent, there are several steps you can take to minimize some of the prejudices your child might experience. First, accept your child as a unique and special person. Your child's feelings that she is seen as a person who has specific qualities can help her to view others as unique individuals. Whenever possible, provide your child with opportunities to interact with people of different backgrounds and cultures. Children can learn a great deal about other people through exposure. *Sesame Street* is a children's television program that has taken specific steps to support cultural diversity.

Point out to your child that the ways people are similar are more important than the ways they are different. The fact that all human beings are born with the ability to think, love, and experience feelings is more fundamental than the color of their skin or where they were born. Our focus tends to be on differences rather than similarities. Helping children to see these similarities may also help us to direct our attention away from the differences as well.

Most children will question why people are different. Help your child learn to value diversity by regarding the differences in culture, appearance, and religion as distinctions that add interest and variety to our world. There are many children's books that explain different types of celebrations for the various holidays and feasts that occur. It is also important to point out and discuss the achievements of outstanding individuals in all groups of people.

Identify the misconceptions, and correct them. Children often hear things from their peers that they take as truth. It is important to find out what incorrect information your child has. In language that can be easily understood by a five year old, explain why the information is wrong. For many children, school is their first exposure to people of different backgrounds. If they have been given misinformation, they carry it to school with them. This is often seen when children encounter a person with a physical handicap. Depending on the information they have, this person may be thought of as "retarded" or even be the target of cruel teasing.

Help your child to become more sensitive to the feelings of others in any situation. Whether it is general name calling or a stereotype based on religion or nationality, guide your child in her understanding of how these words hurt other people. When your child has a good understanding that prejudice and discrimination are unfair, she may be able to create positive change. For a five year old, this may consist of telling another child that it is wrong to tease or being the first on the block to make friends with a new child in the neighborhood. If these things can start at age five, perhaps more of the prejudices we see as adults will start to disappear.

22

DEALING WITH VIOLENCE

There is no doubt in anyone's mind that we live in a world in which violence has become commonplace. Whether we pick up a newspaper or turn on the television, it is quite likely that we will read or see something with violent overtones. Cartoons, movies, TV shows, and other forms of entertainment are often violent in nature. Although this was also the case with the shows and cartoons we might have watched as children (take a look at Bugs Bunny or Road Runner cartoons), we did not have the added impact of the everyday violence going on around us that is so common today. In many areas of the country we read about people shooting other people as they drive on the freeway or 12 year olds bringing guns into school with them. The newspapers are packed full of stories about bombings or kidnappings and murders. Even if you are able to shelter your child from some of the TV shows or news, you may still have to contend with the violence depicted on video games.

There is no doubt that television violence (including news reports) is hazardous to the well-being of children. Not only does it tend to desensitize them to the pain that others may feel, but it also teaches a very dangerous lesson. The violence viewed by children suggests that it is normal and acceptable to resolve conflicts by using fists, guns, karate chops, or whatever else may be available at the time.

Given the place of violence in today's society, is there any way to counter its effects on young children? Talking to your child about what is good and what is not good is the first and most important step. Children need to hear from their role models why it's not good to use your fists to solve a conflict or seek revenge when someone mistreats you. This again brings up the role of modeling in helping children to grow up to be well-adjusted individuals. If they see their parents resolving conflicts by talking and if they are given that guidance, this is the lesson they learn. If, on the other hand, they are guided to stand up for their rights by using their fists or are subjected to Mom or Dad hitting them when they are angry, this is the lesson they learn. Similarly, watching TV with your child and pointing out the good ways characters are handling conflicts as well as the bad ways helps your child to make the distinction on his own.

Being with your child when he watches TV also allows you to monitor his reaction. If you see your child showing discomfort during a TV show, encourage him to change the channel. If the show depicts violence, change the channel even if your child does not appear to be uncomfortable. If you unknowingly go to a movie that has violent overtones, get up and leave. Explain to your child why you are leaving so he understands that this is something you are not willing to accept as entertainment.

Make sure that you can supervise your child's selection of TV shows, movies, tapes, and video games. Although you cannot protect your child from everything, you can monitor what he watches or plays in your house. Read TV listings or movie reviews before making a decision about whether they are acceptable for your child. These may not always accurately reflect the content of the show, but you should get enough information to make an informed decision. Make use of video tapes for programs that are appropriate for five year olds. Either renting or taping from the TV allows you to be certain that what your child is watching is acceptable to you.

Video games are another source of concern for many parents. Some movie stores now offer video games for rent. This allows you to preview specific games your child may wish to buy. As much as you may control what video games your child has, he may be exposed to other games at a friend's house. You can speak to the other parents about which games you allow your child to play. Some parents may be responsive to this, but others may not.

It is also important to remember that children can also be exposed to violence incidentally. Be cautious when watching the news or other TV shows while your child is playing in the same area. Although he may not actually be sitting and watching with you, he may still be listening or watching while he is playing.

The bottom line on violence is that we cannot protect our children from it all the time. We can limit their exposure, however, with the hope of preventing them from becoming too desensitized to the violence in the world around us.

23

FRIENDSHIPS— HOW MANY ARE ENOUGH?

Childhood friendships are developed in stages, beginning with parallel play in toddlerhood. During this stage, playmates are viewed simply as others who are there to play with the same group of toys. As children develop, their perspective shifts from "me" to "them" as they begin to see another person's point of view.

Between the ages of three and seven, friendships exist for today. A friend is someone with whom your child is playing at that particular moment or with whom she plays frequently. If you ask a child of this age to describe her friend, the description is usually in terms of appearance or the type or number of toys she owns. At this stage, there is really no idea that a friendship means a relationship. "Best" friends might change from day to day, and many children play better with two or three children than with a large group.

The understanding of friendship as a relationship begins to emerge between the ages of four and nine. A friend may now be defined as someone who does things that please them. There is still no understanding of the reciprocal nature of friendship until the ages of 6 to 12. At these ages, children will finally have a basic understanding of the give-and-take nature of friendships.

There is no magic number of friends a child should have. Some children go through life with one or two close friends; others have so many friends, they can't keep track. Depending on your child's personality, she may have many or few friends. Do not be concerned unless you start to see consistent difficulties with making or keeping friends.

What do you do about the child who is unpopular or doesn't seem to have any friends? Most children have already learned that relationships are pleasurable. This is something that takes place early in infancy, when they develop a secure relationship with their parent or caregiver. For some children, however, this was not learned. Children who were difficult infants, colicky and irritable, may not have experienced that sense of pleasure and security. It is important to encourage this child to develop a special relationship with at least one friend. Sometimes this means scheduling and arranging activities that are pleasurable for your child. If, as you observe your child interacting with others, you notice behaviors that may alienate her from friends, gently point them out to her. Sometimes just having the knowledge that she is doing something others don't like and the benefits of some constructive criticism on how to change those behaviors are enough. When your child begins school and you meet new parents, arranging times when all of you are together may be a helpful stepping stone to a new friendship. For children who are having difficulty establishing a friendship, knowing that Mom and Dad are supportive can be the best security they need.

If your child continues to have difficulty making friends after you have attempted to set up positive experiences for your child or have worked to identify and correct alienating behaviors, you may wish to seek out a group counseling situation that specifically deals with teaching social skills. You might check with the personnel in your school for a referral to counseling centers that offer such groups. Sometimes, hearing the same suggestions from a different person and having the ability to "practice" under safe conditions makes all the difference in the world to the child who has been struggling to make friends.

What about the child who is too popular? Some children have a natural ability to attract friends. This is generally not a negative quality but it can be of some concern when your child is flooded with invitations, phone calls, and requests for play dates. This can be overwhelming for a child who does not know how to handle her popularity.

It is important to let your child know that although it is very nice to be popular, she does not need to feel obligated to play with everyone or go to each and every birthday party. If your child is concerned about hurting another child's feelings, she may need your help and guidance. Help your child find the words to nicely turn down an invitation without hurting anyone's feelings. Other children may need more adult direction in deciding which invitations to accept and which to turn down.

If your child is popular with her peers, it is important to help her understand that this is something that should not be taken for granted. Learning to appreciate the joys of friendship is a skill that will last your child a lifetime.

24

CAN SIBLINGS EVER GET ALONG?

Siblings seem to be committed to the mutual goal of irritating, annoying, and aggravating each other. It doesn't matter if they are two sisters, two brothers, or a brother and sister. It doesn't matter if they are one year apart, three years apart, or five years apart. They still fight. It may not be all the time. It may not always be a physical fight. But they will fight!

The conflict between siblings is usually a function of the power struggle that exists as they each search for attention, identity, and self-esteem. The fact is that more than one child means competition for the attention of busy parents. The frustration a child feels over lack of parental attention is often quickly and easily directed at a brother or sister.

There are, however, many positives to having a brother or sister that your children may not yet appreciate. Having a sibling helps a child learn how to make friends. They learn to share and negotiate in play situations. Socially, children with siblings may have an easier time being part of a group in which attention must be shared. Additionally, a brother or sister can provide comfort and support in times of stress.

How do you get through the times when they seem to be at each other all day long? If a situation gets out of hand and there is physical fighting, separating your children to different parts of the house should be the immediate solution. Ignore the day-to-day bickering that occurs, or try to help your children come to a compromise.

Unless you actually see one child doing something wrong, don't take sides in their arguments. Part of the rivalry comes from the need to have complete parental support. Try to set aside time to spend with each child alone.

Set up situations that foster cooperation. Special tasks around the house that require the help of all family members can get siblings to work together. Caring for a family pet or working together to save money to buy a special game are a few more suggestions.

Setting clear limits about how your children treat each other is important. Although sibling rivalry may be the norm, being mean and hurtful to another person is not acceptable behavior. A family meeting can serve as a forum for your children to resolve their disagreements. Set aside a specific time for the family to meet to discuss the conflicts they may have with other family members.

We want our children to be friends. In most situations this happens—someday. Until then, it is important to keep reminding yourself that sibling rivalry is a common, temporary situation that affects most families.

Here are some other suggestions that may help reduce the fighting that goes on among siblings.

- Riding in a car can be torture for parents when their children are in the backseat arguing. When you go on a trip (long or short), bring along things to break up the monotony and keep your children focused on something besides each other. Have each child bring a tape recorder (with headphones, of course!) and tapes. Books, simple maps to follow the route, and materials for drawing can help keep children occupied and out of each other's hair!

- It is important to respect your children's privacy. If possible, allow children to have separate rooms. If children need to share a room, use a room divider or bookcase to provide some personal space. Allow each child to have a drawer with a lock or a cabinet where each can keep his or her personal or special items.

- Whenever possible, allow children to work through their own conflicts. When parents intervene, children are left feeling frustrated because they were unable to reach their own resolution to the problem. If you don't want to listen to them argue, ask them to take their fight to another part of the house. If that cannot be accomplished, move yourself to a part of the house where you can't hear them arguing.

- Respect your children's uniqueness. Remember that each child has different personality characteristics and different ways of handling situations. Make every attempt to avoid comparing one child with the other. This will help your children get along better with each other as well as with you.

25

FOSTERING EMPATHY

U nderlying most interactions with other people is our ability to be *empathetic*, to put ourselves in another person's shoes and experience something in the same way they would. Children, at a very young age, have the ability to be empathetic with the feelings of others. Watching a child as young as 18 months of age react to his mother's distress by putting his head on her lap or patting her arm is an early sign of empathy. If they are not encouraged to develop empathy, however, children lose their capacity to be sensitive to others.

When children are as young as two or three, they can empathize with basic feelings, such as happiness, sadness, and anger. These feelings are familiar from their own experiences and easy for them to label. When children are unable to label more complicated emotions, empathy falters. Even though children have experienced such feelings as frustration and embarrassment, they have not learned to label them. For example, if your five year old spills paint all over his clothes, the other children will probably laugh instead of empathize with his embarrassment. Even though they have experienced their own embarrassment at one time or another, they are not yet able to identify and label the feeling.

The capacity to understand fully what another person is feeling does not develop until after age six. To help your child, reinforce along the way any incident of empathetic behavior you see. When you see your child offer a toy to another child who is distressed over losing his, point out how good both he and his friend must have felt by that behavior. Help your child to identify more complicated emotions by labeling them for him. When he can't get a puzzle to fit together and pushes it aside, help him identify his feelings with a statement like, "I know it is frustrating when things don't go together right, but if you keep trying, it might work." Talking about your own emotions is another way of fostering empathy in your child. When you are upset or frustrated, identify these feelings for your child. Explaining why you are feeling a certain way also helps increase his awareness of different emotions.

Being able to empathize with your own child's feelings is another step that helps both you and your child. When your child experiences your ability to empathize with what he is feeling, this serves as a good model for him in his interactions with others. For you, being able to empathize with your child's feelings may help you to understand a little better what's going on in his life. If, for example, your child comes home complaining that he did not get invited to a birthday party, empathize with these feelings instead of rationalizing them with a statement like, "That's okay. They'll be other parties." You may find out that there are other issues at stake. He may have just had a fight with his "best" friend, and the birthday party was an added factor. Perhaps this is a popular child whom all the children would like to have as a friend. Whatever the situation, being able to empathize with your child may open up a whole new source of sharing between the two of you.

26

THE COMPETITIVE WORLD OF SPORTS

Many children around the age of five are introduced to the world of organized sports. There is no question that regular physical activity is essential to physical well-being and health. It is important that young children become early participants in a lifestyle that leads to healthy habits as adults. Physical activity helps develop eye-hand coordination as well as muscle coordination and tone. Organized sports can provide children with an early opportunity to be part of a group and learn to cooperate with others. How do you know whether your child is ready for organized sports?

The first criterion should be your child's desire to participate in a particular sport. As parents, we must ask ourselves if we are encouraging a particular sport because *we* want our child to participate or because our child is expressing an interest. It is one thing to encourage children to try a new and unfamiliar activity, but they should always be given the option to stop a sport if they find it is not something they like. Children at this age are often afraid to disappoint their parents by telling them that they do not like a certain activity, especially if Mom or Dad is especially enthusiastic about it. Parents should try to tune in to the unspoken signals given by children. Such behaviors as finding excuses for not being ready for practices and games or getting involved in a different activity just as it's time to leave may be your child's way of showing her reluctance to be involved in a particular sport.

Second, consideration should be given to your child's physical abilities. Children in this age group begin to compare themselves with peers in academic areas, social groups, and physical attributes. Many children need help placing their body images in perspective, especially if they are overweight or not well coordinated. Giving children an opportunity to participate in a sport regardless of their physical coordination is a wonderful idea that should be encouraged.

Attention should also be given, however, to what may occur if a child is unable to keep up with others. Sometimes pursuing a sport that does not place your child in a group situation is a better first start for those children who are not able to keep up or who may be concerned with how they look in comparison with their peers. Individual sports, such as swimming (noncompetitive), jogging, martial arts, cycling, or skiing, can improve physical coordination but allow children to work at their own pace and, essentially, compete with themselves. Swimming, jogging, and skiing are also great activities in which family members can participate together.

It is important to make a distinction between providing encouragement for your child's athletic ability and putting pressure on her to succeed. Parents can encourage participation in sports by making sure the necessary knowledge, training, and equipment are available. Children also need their parents to help them develop realistic expectations about their athletic abilities. Children who aim too high, either because of their own expectations or in response to their parents' enthusiasm, can end up being disappointed and dissatisfied with their performance. It is very easy for parents to put pressure on the young child who displays an innate talent early on. There will come a point, however, when peers may catch up and perform equally as well or better. For the child who has been told "You're the best" or "You do better than the big kids," this can have a serious effect on her self-esteem.

Competition can be positive when it encourages children to perform their best. Overcompetitiveness develops when an emphasis is placed on winning above all else. If your child plays a team sport, attempt to focus on individual performances and fun rather than on who won or lost the game. Monitor your own reaction to competition both as an observer and as a participant. If children see their parents engaged in highly competitive behaviors, they will model those same behaviors. Finally, watch for early signs of overcompetitiveness: unusually intense and prolonged periods of anger or depression after a loss, tantrums on the playing field, and extreme nervousness. If you see your child demonstrating any of these behaviors, help your child put things in perspective by reinforcing the fact that it is a game and the goal is to have fun. If your child continues to show signs of overcompetitiveness, it may be necessary to take a break from the sport for a short time and try another, less competitive activity.

If your child is interested in a team sport, those that are grouped according to developmental level rather than age are generally better for younger children. Specific group sports that are appropriate for five-year-old children are discussed in the next key.

27

ORGANIZED SPORTS

I f your child is ready for and interested in an organized, group sport, which is the best or most appropriate? Some children express an interest in a particular sport because their friends or classmates are becoming involved in it. Other children may need more outside encouragement to try a specific sport or activity. Again, children should be encouraged but not pushed into trying a sport. It is not beneficial either to you or to your child if guilt over disappointing Mom or Dad becomes the motivating factor.

Many school districts and neighborhood groups begin peewee soccer and T-ball at the five-year-old level. Soccer promotes teamwork, builds endurance and body coordination, and provides aerobic conditioning. Soccer tends to attract more gregarious types who like group activities. It can also be good for less talented athletes because it allows children to participate in a team sport without being singled out for their performance.

Soccer is a good sport for both girls and boys, and in some areas, younger aged teams are mixed gender. Parents are often able to volunteer as coaches, which can provide a good opportunity for time spent together. Whether parents participate as coaches or observers, they must maintain the fine balance between encouraging their child to participate and have fun and criticizing their child for not meeting parental expectations.

T-ball is a more competitive sport and generally attracts children who have good self-esteem and are comfortable with individual attention. T-ball is a modified version of baseball in which children hit a ball from a stationary tee rather than face a pitcher. It requires good eye-hand coordination, strength, and agility. Children who are not well coordinated or who feel uncomfortable in the spotlight may have difficulty with this sport. An important factor for all children, especially those who are less physically coordinated, is the team makeup. Grouping children by ability level is important in T-ball so that the less coordinated child does not feel that he is the only one who can't hit or catch the ball. Unfortunately, children even as young as age five can be very cruel in what they say to others. The last thing parents want for their children is to have them start to believe that they aren't as good as or can't keep up with their peers!

Gymnastics is an excellent fitness activity that promotes strength, flexibility, body control, and self-discipline. Although this is an individual sport similar to martial arts or swimming, gymnastics can be highly competitive and is best for children who are comfortable having their performance observed. Children, especially girls, who have concerns about body image or coordination may have difficulty with gymnastics. Here again, concern about grouping is essential. Children should not be placed in a group or class in which the majority of the children are on a different level. As in every activity role models are important, but too diverse an ability level can set children up for their own perceived "failure" in keeping up with what the other children are doing.

What about the child who has no interest in any type of sport or activity? How much should parents "push" to get a child involved? Modeling is the most important thing parents can do to encourage physical activity. Children learn at a very early age that physical activity is not important if they see Mom and Dad as sedentary people. If they see that physical activity is important to the whole family, however, they are more likely to incorporate physical activity as a part of the daily routine. Even if you are not physically active, a daily walk around the block or a family bike ride can provide some motivation for the child who is not interested in sports or physical activities. In addition to providing suggestions for different activities, it is sometimes helpful to find a friend who is already involved in a sport to provide encouragement. This can be one of the positive aspects of peer pressure!

A final word of caution to all well-meaning parents: This is a time of your child's life when you should be able to truly enjoy his or her experiences and exposure to new activities. Most five year olds are still fairly uncoordinated and have not yet learned how to function as part of an organized group. Allowing them to go onto a soccer field or baseball field and have a good time is the best gift you can give your child. Too often, parents become caught up in the competitive aspect of sports and expect their young children to perform at a level far above their developmental levels. Parents want their children to succeed in whatever they do, but sometimes that success means going out, having a good time, and developing a positive self-image without being the best player on the team!

28

IS YOUR CHILD READY FOR KINDERGARTEN?

If your child's birthday happens to fall during the latter half of the year, you may be one of the many parents wrestling with the question of readiness for starting kindergarten. Across the nation, cutoff dates for starting kindergarten vary substantially. Some states have coordinated the date with the start of the school year (September). In others the cutoff date is the end of December, and still others use July 1 as a cutoff. Even within a state, school districts can vary so that children may be eligible to start kindergarten in school district A but would have an additional year if they live across the street in school district B. The closer your child's birthday to the cutoff date established by your school district, the more concerned you may be about making the right decision.

The two most common reasons for considering delaying a child's entrance into kindergarten focus on a general level of immaturity and an overall delay in development. It is important to realize that a lack of maturity in comparison with age peers does not mean your child is not ready for kindergarten. Children mature at different rates and in different areas. If social immaturity is the issue, interactions with peers who are more mature may be exactly what your child needs. Holding back your child and providing interactions with children who are one year younger may defeat the purpose. If you see your child as immature in a specific area, how will her other abilities be challenged? A child who is socially immature but average to above average in cognitive skills and language development needs to be in an environment that provides activities that challenge these other skill areas.

Overall delays in development may be a valid reason for considering delayed entrance into kindergarten. If your child is delayed in language, cognitive, physical, and social development and has a late birthday, spending another year in an appropriately stimulating prekindergarten program *may* be beneficial to her self-esteem. However, it is extremely difficult at this age level to determine whether delays are truly developmental (suggesting that these skills will eventually catch up) or the forerunners of a specific learning disability. The decision to delay entrance into kindergarten is often a judgment call you should make only after carefully considering all the options and discussing them with the people who are involved with your child.

If your child has been involved in a preschool program, the first person to contact is her preschool teacher. The observations of the person who has worked with your child (along with numerous other four to five year olds) provide valuable information about classroom performance, social interactions, and overall readiness for kindergarten.

In addition to talking with your child's present classroom teacher, contact with personnel in your school district is essential. Does the school district have a philosophy on delayed entrance into kindergarten? How flexible is the curriculum to adapt to differences among typical children? Are any additional services available (speech therapy or contact with special education teachers, for example) if your child should need them? What is the percentage of children in kindergarten who are identified as having difficulty in specific areas? What is the focus of the kindergarten curriculum? Some schools work from the assumption that all children have had preschool experience and therefore provide an academically oriented curriculum. Other schools view kindergarten as a child's first exposure to formal education and design a curriculum geared toward socialization skills and basic school readiness skills (separating from Mom or Dad, completing tabletop activities, and working within a group). These questions can be answered by speaking with the principal or, if possible, a current kindergarten teacher.

If you suspect developmental delays early, the first step is to contact your pediatrician to rule out problems with vision or hearing. A formal evaluation by a psychologist and/or speech and language therapist experienced with young children can also provide information that will be helpful in making a decision. If, after formalized testing, areas of deficit are identified, consideration should be given to support services in kindergarten. These services may include placement in a special education kindergarten class, which has a smaller number of children, and a special education teacher who is trained to teach to a child's learning style.

29

HOW CHILDREN LEARN

A ccording to Swiss psychologist Jean Piaget, children are programmed to learn and practice. A child's cognitive development occurs in stages, and according to Piaget's theory, a child cannot advance to a higher stage without acquiring all the information in a lower stage. This developmental theory of intelligence has been widely accepted by many professionals who hold the belief that children innately love to learn. Once a skill is mastered, they are ready to move on to a new skill.

Watch a toddler during his first experience with blocks. Once he is shown that the blocks can be stacked up, he practices this skill over and over. When the skill is fully incorporated into his bank of behaviors, he is ready to move on to a new skill, perhaps making a bridge.

The acquisition of language is another example of practice and mastery. An infant starts out babbling and using gestures to communicate. Through the use of modeling (Mom says "milk" as she holds up the baby bottle) and practice, he eventually acquires the word *milk*. There is now another motivation for learning that occurs. When he says "milk," he is rewarded with a bottle of milk. What a great way to learn! The interactions of a young child with his environment set the stage for learning.

All young children use the vehicle of play to learn about their environment. There are no special requirements for play, it's lots of fun, and children can learn effectively through experimentation. Children engaging in imaginative play in a toy kitchen are learning one-to-one correspondence as they make certain each guest has a plate and napkin. They are learning different categories as they sort the pretend fruits, vegetables, dishes, and silverware. They are also learning responsibility when it is time to clean up and put everything back in its proper place.

Although much of the learning that takes place before a child enters school occurs through experimentation with the environment, parents can encourage learning by providing stimulation. This does not mean that you have to play with your child every minute of the day! Children need to learn to function independent of their parents. It does mean, however, exposing your child to different situations, such as the grocery store, the library, or the neighborhood in general. When you are driving or walking, talk about what you see to help increase vocabulary and concepts. Talk about what your child is doing during play. Ask questions that stimulate thinking and problem-solving skills. For example, when your child is building with blocks, ask what he is building as well as why, who might live there, what they do there, and where you might find a building like that. If your child is drawing a picture, focus on directional concepts, such as top, bottom, right, and left. Help your child expand on pictures of people to include backgrounds. Ask questions like, "What else do you find in a forest [or whatever is being drawn]?"

Children learn a tremendous amount from incidental exposure. If you talk to your child about what you are doing or what you see as you are riding in the car, you will be amazed at the impact it has. When your child expresses an interest in something, listen and respond. Provide the information that is being asked plus a little more. This provides an opening for your child to ask more questions.

You can speed up your child's learning through specific programs or workbooks, but ask yourself an important question: Is it in your child's best interest to do so? If your child is seeking more stimulation and demonstrates a specific ability in reading or mathematics, provide more experience in these areas. If not, allow him to continue at his own pace. Provide the exposure, and he will take in the information as he is ready.

30

THE LOVE OF READING

Reading is the most fundamental skill needed for school success. If you are able to develop a love of reading in your child at an early age, you have set the stage for success in school.

Infants can be exposed to reading. Sitting together and looking at a book is an early step in teaching your child what it is like to read for pleasure. As your child becomes older, allow her to pick out the books that are of interest. Sometimes this may mean reading the same book over ten times! This is okay because it shows that she is making the connection between pictures and print, as well as engaging in something that is enjoyable for her.

When you read aloud with your child, stop and ask questions periodically during the story. This helps develop memory skills and increases comprehension. By using books with lots of illustrations, you can then ask your child to go back and "read" the story to you. Although she is relying totally on the pictures, she is making the connection that a book carries a message.

Let your child see you reading for pleasure and information. Whether books, newspapers, or magazines, it is important to let your child see you spend time reading. You may wish to set up a "reading time" in the evening. Spend some time reading to your child, and use the remainder of the time for individual reading. What great role models you are if your child is exposed to both Mom and Dad reading!

As your five year old begins to develop a basic sight vocabulary, read books, like those by Dr. Seuss, which present rhymes and word families. As you read, point out the different words to her. To foster early reading skills, point out letters of the alphabet to your child. Use alphabet blocks or magnetic letters to help your child spell out words in which she is interested. Make an alphabet letter book, and cut out pictures from magazines that go with each letter. By the time most children enter school, they can recite the alphabet and identify most uppercase letters. Point out letters or words on signs in the neigborhood, or ask your child to find a certain letter.

Encourage drawing and writing skills. As your child "writes" on a page, ask her what it says. By age five, children have a good understanding that the written word has meaning. Allow your child to make her own grocery list and take it to the store with her. Let your child open mail and read it aloud to her.

The knowledge that written words carry a message is the most important skill your child can learn. Each child reads and writes at her own rate. Some children are more interested in reading than others, which affects how quickly they learn. By providing exposure, a stimulating environment, and praise for whatever she is able to do, your child can develop these skills at her own pace.

31

WAYS TO ENHANCE YOUR CHILD'S LEARNING

T hroughout most of the keys in this book, suggestions have been given on how to improve basic skill areas. The most important aspect of learning is to provide for your child an environment that is supportive and stimulating. This does not mean that every child needs to go to expensive camp programs or that children need to be involved in all sorts of activities. Nor does it suggest that you should spend all your time and energy "enriching" your child's environment. By using everyday situations, objects, songs, or books, you can provide plenty of stimulation for your child.

When most children are ready to enter school, they are able to count by rote to 10, 20, or sometimes higher. They have the ability to recognize some numerals and begin to develop some understanding of quantities. You can help to develop number skills by using the toys and items you find in your child's daily environment. As he is playing, help him to count his blocks, dolls, or other toys. When he is helping you in the kitchen or has the chore of setting the table, have him count out the number of napkins, forks, or other utensils needed for all family members. These activities can become part of the daily routine rather than a drill. During dinner, play number games with the pieces of food left on the plate. Have your child count the number of carrots on the plate and say how many will be left if one is eaten.

Singing number songs with your child also helps to improve counting skills. "One-Two-Buckle My Shoe" and "Ten Little Indians" are only two examples. When you are driving in the car, point out numbers to foster recognition. Play a game in which your child must find the "red two" or "green five." This provides an extra clue (color) to help him find the correct numeral.

Most five year olds have a very limited understanding of time concepts. By the time they enter kindergarten, almost all children know their age, and the majority know how old they will be on their next birthday. Less than half are able to tell what day of the week it is, and very few five year olds have the ability to tell time on a clock with hands.

To help children grasp time concepts, it is important to stick to basic routines. This does not mean a rigid schedule, which is almost impossible these days, but a general routine of getting up, dressing, eating breakfast, going to school, doing homework, having dinner, taking a bath, and going to bed. This type of routine helps children to understand "before" and "after," as well as a general time frame for when things happen. Concrete tasks, such as choosing clothes for school the evening before, helps them to grasp the concept of "tomorrow." Five year olds are usually excited to receive a calendar that helps them understand days, weeks, and months. If an event is coming up (birthday or holiday), make a paper chain with a loop for each day. Each night before going to bed, have your child remove a loop and count the remaining ones. Relating time to something commonplace is also helpful to children. If your child is staying with a friend for half an hour, explain that it is as long as his favorite television show.

Developing language concepts is another area that can be worked on in a very casual way. As you are riding in the car with your child, play a guessing game. "I see something big and yellow, with wheels and lots of children inside." Not only are you providing different vocabulary words for your child, but you are also getting her to think and put together concepts.

If your child needs help with the alphabet, play games like "I'm going on a trip and taking an (apple)." Take turns filling in the blank with a word that starts with *a*, then *b*, then *c*, and so on through the alphabet.

As discussed in the previous key, reading is a wonderful way to develop many skill areas. Pointing out words that start with the same letter of your child's name or choosing a letter a week and cutting out pictures from magazines are other ways of solidifying these skills.

Keep in mind that your child will progress at her own pace. There is no need to go out and buy books on readiness skills or other expensive programs. Use the everyday things that occur in his environment to tap into those skills he needs for school.

32

THE WORLD OF COMPUTERS

Most children, if they haven't yet had experience with computers, will probably be introduced to computers when they enter school. Schools use computers to foster mathematics concepts as well as writing, language, and reading skills. Many families also have some type of computer in their homes. If you choose not to own a computer, rest assured that your child will not suffer. Most schools can provide sufficient experience to make most children computer literate.

If you own or plan to own a computer, it is important to focus on several factors related to choosing software. Computers should be viewed as an educational tool that can be used to supplement a child's formal education. They should not be viewed as glorified Nintendo games to be used for entertainment.

Before choosing a software program for your child, it is important to try it first. Make sure there is a return policy, or see if you can preview the program before purchasing it. If you buy a program that does not hold your child's interest or is not appropriate for your child's developmental level, it will be useless.

Even though the focus of programs should be educational, they can still be fun and entertaining. If a program does not catch your child's interest, it loses its educational value. Interaction and exploration are other qualities to watch for.

A program that is open ended allows children to continue to build on past experiences every time they use the program.

Programs for younger children should be responsive (not a long wait for feedback) and should direct children to correct responses in a way that is interesting and fun. If a program simply beeps for wrong answers without giving some direction toward a correct response, your child begins to feel incompetent and frustrated. Try to choose programs that give children something to do beyond the computer. Some writing programs give children the opportunity to make banners, signs, cards, or other things they can color or play with.

Stay involved with what your child is doing on the computer. Work with your child to explore new features in a program, or sit down and actually play a game with him. See if the program has difficulty levels that can be adjusted for an older child or as your child becomes an expert. Try to find programs that are useful over a wide age range. Younger and older children can use the same program in very different ways and be very successful.

Resources are available to help you evaluate programs. The Computer Learning Foundation is a nonprofit organization that encourages technology in education. Just as with television shows, movies, and video games, watch the content of computer programs for characters you may not want your child to copy. A recent evaluation of computer programs found very minimal examples of violence or sexual stereotypes, but they found subtle stereotyping in the form of outdated stereotypes and gender bias. Although it is reassuring to know that this does not occur with much frequency, it is still important to keep in mind as you search for appropriate software.

33

PROVIDING CHALLENGES FOR YOUR GIFTED CHILD

T he information provided in this book has been focused on the typical five-year-old child, but what about the child who has skills beyond those of the typical child? What about the child who began to talk at a very early age and, by age three or four, had started to develop reading skills? There are children who show specific abilities well beyond their chronologic age.

Children can be considered "gifted" based on an overall level of advanced development, or they may have a talent in a very specific area. Each of us believes our child is the smartest in the world; however, it is important to assess her skills objectively without the interference of our personal feelings. Formalized testing is often the only way to determine if a child truly is intellectually gifted. Tests, such as the Stanford Binet Intelligence Scale IV, the Wechsler Preschool and Primary Scale of Intelligence R, and the Wechsler Intelligence Scale for Children III, are standardized measures administered by a licensed psychologist that provide an IQ (intelligence quotient) score. These tests indicate whether your child is functioning intellectually at a level above her peers. They do not indicate, however, if your child is talented in a particular area, such as music. For this, you may have to arrange for a consultation with a music teacher or other qualified person.

If you suspect that your child is gifted, the first area to explore is the level of stimulation she is able to receive in her current environment. Some teachers are very tuned-in to children's abilities and provide challenges within the classroom setting. Other children are quite content with advanced reading material from the library or participation in extra activities beyond preschool or kindergarten.

If, on the other hand, your child is not stimulated in her current environment, you may wish to pursue a specific program that promotes further skill development.

Some school districts have programs for gifted and talented children that start as early as kindergarten. You can contact your school district to find out whether such a program is available and what steps you should take to refer your child. If your district provides a program, they will most likely want to complete an evaluation if one has not already been done.

If your school district does not provide a program for kindergarten students and you are interested in providing an enrichment program, you may have to pursue something privately. This can range from a private school specifically for gifted students to Saturday or afterschool programs that provide additional challenges. Some of these programs may be run through a local university.

One factor to consider when determining whether your child needs a special program is the degree of contact with her typical peers. This age level is a crucial time for the development of social skills and friendships. Some children who are intellectually gifted may be immature socially. As a parent, it is important to weigh the benefits of intellectual stimulation against the benefits of social development. Depending on the level of your child's abilities, it may be more beneficial to provide additional stimulation at home or after school while maintaining regular school placement and contact with peers. We all wish our children to be well-rounded individuals. Too much focus on one particular area can disrupt the balance of experiences needed to foster overall development.

34

PREPARING FOR SCHOOL

A s your five year old gets ready to enter kindergarten, there is a mixture of excitement and anxiety. For many families, it is the child who is excited and the parents who are anxious! There are, however, many children who may be anxious about the start of school. For these children, this may be their first experience with daily separation from home. Concerns about fitting in, meeting new friends, meeting a new teacher, finding the classroom, or, more important, finding the bathroom may be weighing on your child's mind.

Before the start of school, talk with your child about the experiences he may have. Some schools have kindergarten orientation in which the children go into school to see the classroom and meet the teacher. As you try to assess your child's reaction, see whether you can also identify areas of concern. Instead of asking your child directly about his concerns, address the concerns in a casual way. Saying something like, "I heard from Bobby's mom that there is someone who meets all the kindergarten children at the bus and takes them to the classroom" may alleviate concerns about having to find the classroom alone.

If your school does not have an orientation, arrange with the building principal to bring your child for a tour of the building before the start of school. Most schools are open the week before school begins and should be willing to allow you to come in. You may even get lucky and find the teacher setting up the classroom!

Try to find out who some of the other children will be in your child's class. If possible, arrange a play date with a child before the start of school. It is very comforting for a child to know someone he can connect with in a new situation. Seeing that familiar face and, sometimes, knowing that someone else has similar concerns can ease the discomfort of a new situation.

Depending on your child's personality, you must decide whether you want to play up or play down the start of school. If your child is highly anxious, you may want to treat everything in a very casual fashion. When you go out to buy new school clothes, mention only why you are buying them. Treat the school orientation or visit in a relaxed way. Have your child share the information with others only if he chooses to do so.

If, on the other hand, your child is very comfortable with the idea of going to school, you may want to treat this like the exciting event it is. Make a special trip to buy those school clothes, and show them off when you get home. Talk about the school visit, the classroom, and the teacher so your child feels your excitement as well.

Many parents want to be at school when their child arrives on the first day. Whether you take your child to school or follow the bus and meet him there, it is important to make your good-bye short and matter of fact. Some children do quite well until they see Mom or Dad at the school building. The anxieties that were kept under control may now come to the surface. A quick "Good-bye, I love you, have a great day, and I'll see you later" is the best approach. Any anxieties your child may feel outside the building will soon be gone when he gets inside and realizes that school is a safe, fun place to be.

Presenting a positive attitude about school is the best thing you can do for your child. Associate school with independence, growing up, and learning new things. Help your child treat school as an adventure, and encourage your child to "play school" at home. This often helps to alleviate any underlying fears or concerns that may be present.

Be supportive of your child by providing extra attention and reassurance. Encourage your child to talk about school, friends, and new situations. Show interest in what your child is doing and saying about school. Try to make your home into a learning environment. Set aside 15 minutes for reading out loud, and make sure school projects and pictures are proudly displayed on the refrigerator door. Give your child his own calendar to mark special events that are happening at school.

This is also a time when it is important to encourage autonomy. The more your child is dependent on you for fulfilling his needs or feelings of security, the greater difficulty he will have separating from you. If your child has not had preschool experience, start to gradually increase the time your child can separate from you before school actually begins. Make use of familiar babysitters or family members to foster independence from you.

Finally, remember that temporary behavior changes are very common during the first two months of kindergarten. Children often show signs of increased dependence on Mom or Dad, uncooperative behavior, or regressive behaviors such as crying or bed wetting. As children become more accustomed to the new change in their lives, these behaviors dissipate. If it helps, check in with other parents who went through this stage for the reassurance that this too will pass!

35

I WON'T GO TO SCHOOL

Periodically during the course of your child's school career, you will be faced with, "I won't go to school." There may be a clear, identifiable reason for this attitude, or you may not have any idea where this is coming from.

Anxiety is often the root of a sudden reluctance to attend school. Children who have had a negative experience with a friend may have the fear that it will happen again or that other children won't like them. Sometimes the anxiety is not related to school but is focused on something happening at home. This is often seen if a family member has been ill or there has been a death in the family.

Other times the refusal to go to school is simply related to a concern that they will miss something special at home. If a sibling is sick and staying home, there is always reason to question what special things might be happening. If Grandma and Grandpa have come for a visit, children often want to stay home to spend time with them. At age five, children don't always have a good concept of time and may not understand that Grandma and Grandpa will be staying for two weeks.

Whatever the reason for your child refusing to go to school, there are several steps you can take. First, make it very clear to your child that you will discuss the reasons but that she still has to go to school. There should be no negotiations on this point. Take the time to talk with your child about the problems and help come up with solutions. By addressing the reason together, you can often brainstorm a number of solutions, some of which may be effective.

If the problem becomes persistent and you are unable to identify a reason, talk to your child's teacher. Sometimes children are unwilling to discuss the real reason out of embarrassment. The classroom teacher may be able to shed some light on the problem. Even if the teacher indicates that your child appears perfectly happy at school, check to see if anything might be happening on the bus or at recess. Sometimes children don't make their feelings known at school but react at home. If everything seems to be all right in school, look carefully at the home situation to see whether there is any cause for anxiety or fear there.

If your child frequently reports being sick, have her checked by the pediatrician. If your pediatrician gives a clean bill of health, you may want to consider anxiety as the cause of the illness. Some children feel better once they get into school and realize that their fears are unfounded. Work with the school personnel to set up a system for getting your child to school. Perhaps she can spend a little time in the nurse's office or another comfortable spot until her anxiety passes and she is able to go into class.

Other children may have the idea that they will be able to play and have fun with Mom if they stay home from school. If you are not certain your child is truly sick and you allow her to stay home, make sure that she stays in bed, without television and without playing. This often cures the mysterious morning illness!

The most important factor to remember, and the most difficult thing to do, is to make it clear that your child *must* go to school. It is very difficult to see your young child upset, but allowing her to stay home can set up an unhealthy pattern of behavior. Maintain a matter-of-fact attitude about going to school, and put on a positive face. School is one of the first major responsibilities your child will have to deal with, so it's important to get off to a good start. Reassure her that you will be home when school is over, give her a kiss and a cheery "Have a great day!" and send her on her way. If necessary, give the school a quick call to reassure yourself that your child is okay!

36

ATTENTION DEFICIT / HYPERACTIVITY DISORDER IN THE FIVE YEAR OLD

Attention Deficit/Hyperactivity Disorder (ADHD) is a term often used in describing school-age children. When children enter the school environment and are required to sit in a seat and attend to auditory directions with 20 or more other five year olds around them, difficulties with attending skills often become apparent. The child who has difficulty following directions or waiting his turn or who acts differently from peers is often identified first by a kindergarten teacher as a child who may have ADHD. What exactly is ADHD, and how many children are actually identified with this disorder?

ADHD is defined by the *Diagnostic and Statistical Manual IV* (DSM-IV) as a disorder characterized by two basic symptoms: inattention and hyperactivity-impulsivity. These symptoms can also be seen in combination. Onset is before age seven and has a duration of at least six months. Difficulties from these symptoms are present in two or more settings, and there is evidence of impairment in social, academic, or occupational functioning.

Inattention can be seen in children who make careless mistakes in schoolwork, have difficulty sustaining their attention, appear not to listen to directions, or have difficulty following instructions. They often fail to complete activities, are disorganized and "scattered," are easily distracted by other things around them, and interrupt tasks to attend to minor noises or events that are easily ignored by others. Daily activities can be easily forgotten, and inattention can be seen in difficulty in following a conversation or rules in a game. If six or more of these symptoms are displayed, the diagnosis would be considered ADHD, Predominantly Inattentive Type.

Fidgety, squirmy, out-of-seat behavior is often a manifestation of hyperactive behavior. Excessive running or climbing in situations that are inappropriate (for example, church or school), difficulty engaging in "quiet" activities, and excessive talking are also signs of hyperactivity. Children who are unable to wait their turn and who interrupt and blurt out answers may be displaying signs of impulsive behaviors. Six or more of these symptoms would meet the criteria for ADHD, Predominantly Hyperactive-Impulsive Type.

Upon close examination, many of these "symptoms" would be typical characteristics if you were observing a two-year-old child. What is normal behavior for a toddler, however, becomes a significant problem for the three to five percent of children who are eventually diagnosed with ADHD. Their impulsivity, inattention, and hyperactive behaviors can often lead to difficulties in school and social problems. They also present a significant strain for parents who try to deal with an unmanageable child.

111

Children with ADHD are often labeled early on as "bad" kids whose parents have little control over their behavior. They often have difficulty in nursery school because they can't follow a routine or have difficulty interacting with peers. At home, these children may not be able to sit at the table long enough to eat dinner or may be seen switching from one toy to another until every toy has been taken out of the closet. Yet parents often report that their child can sit for extended periods of time if they are interested in a video or playing a Nintendo game. This is not unusual and is often very typical of ADHD children. In a new setting, on a one-to-one basis, or when involved in an interesting activity, signs of ADHD may be minimal or absent.

A diagnosis of ADHD should only be made after ruling out other possible causes, including medical, emotional, and environmental variables that can cause similar symptoms. A multidisciplinary evaluation should incorporate findings from medical examinations; psychological, educational, and speech and language testing; behavioral rating scales completed by both teacher and parents, and a neurological evaluation.

Such characteristics as inattentiveness, impulsivity, and underachievement can also be seen in non-ADHD children who may suffer from emotional difficulties, such as depression or anxiety. A differential diagnosis, using the results of the multidisciplinary evaluation, is therefore essential before an effective treatment plan can be put into place.

37

TREATING ADHD IN THE FIVE-YEAR-OLD CHILD

If you have had your child evaluated and it has been determined that she has Attention Deficit/Hyperactivity Disorder, the next step is to put a treatment program into place. Treatments for ADHD run the spectrum from special diets that eliminate food additives and sugar to medications, such as psychostimulants and antidepressants. Just as the diagnosis of ADHD must be multimodal, the treatment should also be multimodal to be maximally effective.

The first and most important approach in treating ADHD is a combination of counseling and behavior management. Children need to learn about ADHD and work on increasing their self-esteem. Before being identified as having ADHD, many children have been in trouble at school or have had negative interactions with significant adults in their lives. It is extremely important that they understand that they are not "bad" children because of the way they behave.

Families also need to learn about ADHD and behavior management techniques to use at home. Reducing the amount of stimulation in the immediate environment, making eye contact when giving directions, and providing follow-up to make sure that tasks are completed are all ways parents can help their child with ADHD.

A therapist or counselor who is well versed in ADHD can also work with the school to recommend modifications to the classroom that can assist the child with ADHD. Surrounding a child with good role models, giving out one direction or task at a time, and having a set consequence for specific behaviors are modifications that can be made within a regular classroom environment. Preferential seating at the front of the room may be helpful to keep a child on-task. If your child's teacher has limited experience working with children with ADHD, reading materials on ADHD can also be helpful.

Some children with ADHD may also require special education services to remediate learning disabilities. Providing the best environment for a child with ADHD takes tremendous effort from all involved. Many children with ADHD are able to stay in the regular classroom setting. Others, however, may require a smaller grouping and specific remediation to be able to focus better on the academic work being presented.

There is a subset of children with ADHD who may require intervention with psychostimulant medications. The most common medications used to treat ADHD are Ritalin and Cylert. These medications increase the production of a neurotransmitter in the brain that is lacking in children with ADHD. As the neurotransmitter reaches acceptable levels, attention increases.

Many parents are uncomfortable with the thought of "medicating" their child. It is important to understand, however, that some children are unable to reach their full potential without medication. Often these medications are used only when the children are in school so they are able to concentrate more fully. Although there are some minor side effects, the benefits can outweigh them. Careful monitoring by a physician is essential if medication is recommended.

114

Parents of children with ADHD need to know that there are other people out there who face the same challenges as they do. Children and Adults with Attention Deficit Disorder (CHADD) is a national, nonprofit organization created several years ago as a support group for parents. Many chapters provide, in addition to peer support groups, lectures by professionals in the field and a lending library with current information on ADHD and strategies for coping. Being able to share with others the successes as well as the frustrations of raising a child with ADHD is a powerful and essential outlet.

38

SCHOOL CONFERENCES

Your child is in school, everything seems to be going well, and you are now ready for your first teacher conference. What can you expect, and how can or should you prepare for it? Whether your conference is a formality to discuss your child's progress or a special conference arranged because of a specific concern, it is important to prepare what you would like to discuss with the teacher. Most teacher conferences are time limited, which means you must be ready to ask specific questions.

When your child's teacher is giving feedback on your child's classroom performance, try to be objective. If the report is not as positive as you hoped, remember that your child's ability and behavior are not a reflection on you. It is always difficult for parents to hear something less than positive about their child, but if you take the time to listen to what the teacher is saying, you may realize that these are behaviors you also see at home.

Ask the teacher for concrete examples. This helps both you and the teacher to identify how frequently a behavior occurs and whether there are any specific circumstances surrounding it. For example, if your child has difficulty with transitions, you may be able determine that his behavior is problematic only when he is involved in an activity that he really likes. This might help you and the teacher work together to develop a way of dealing with this behavior.

Be an advocate for your child. Even if you believe that your child is being treated unfairly or that the teacher may be overreacting to a particular behavior, try to be constructive in your discussion. Instead of accusing the teacher, try to give suggestions on how best to handle your child's behavior. You know your child better than anyone. Sometimes a problem can be resolved easily through an understanding of how a child reacts to certain situations.

Listen carefully to what your child's teacher is saying, both positive and negative, and restate it. This helps to clarify statements that are made and ensure that you are both on the same track. For example, if the teacher is talking about how well your child is doing in reading, this can mean a number of things. He may be doing well in relation to the other children in the class, he may doing well in relation to his other skills, or he may doing so well he should be challenged in this area. These are three very different statements. Unless you restate what you heard the teacher say, there may be confusion.

If there is a problem that is discussed at your school conference, make every effort to work with the teacher in generating a solution. There must be a cooperative effort between parents and teachers to address many of the different problems that occur in schools today. Provide the teacher with any suggestions you can think of, including methods you may be able to carry over into the home. Sometimes problems are averted by a cooperative effort between both parties.

It is very important, at all stages of development, to share the results of your conference with your child. In general terms, explain what you and the teacher spoke about. If necessary, talk about the particular issues discussed. Present problem behaviors in a nonaccusatory way, and ask your child for help in developing a solution.

If, after completing the conference, you do not feel comfortable with the outcome or still have unanswered questions, do not hesitate to ask the teacher for another meeting. It is important to establish a good working relationship with your child's teacher so that the two of you can work together to ensure your child's school success.

39

PEER RELATIONSHIPS IN SCHOOL

Five-year-old children have reached the stage at which they begin to rate themselves in comparison to others. This comparison may be in terms of physical strength, appearance, or intelligence. Some comparison is internally generated, and some may come from the school system's focus on rating and grades. This can be counteracted when teachers in school stress cooperative efforts in learning situations. Children are required to learn to give and receive with their peers. Flexibility in interpersonal relationships is developed as they learn to yield in some situations and stand their ground in others.

Many children in kindergarten have a best friend. Because they are more capable at having a conversation, they are able to share information about what is going on in their lives. Common interests and similar personalities are two factors that often affect who your child ends up with as a best friend. Some kindergartners are able to work through the temporary spats and misunderstandings that occur on a regular basis. Other children have not developed these skills, and their best friend may change from day to day. In most cases this is one of the developmental steps children must go through before they are able to establish lasting friendships.

Children who have immature social skills or a poor self-concept may have more difficulty with peer relationships and friendships. At five years of age, most problems with peers are expressed through teasing.

Some children may use teasing as a way of establishing themselves within their peer group. If the goal is to be accepted by a particular group, focusing on the vulnerability of others may be a way to establish that membership. If the children in this particular group are teasing another child, there may be considerable pressure on the child seeking acceptance to follow suit.

Other children may use teasing to protect their own vulnerablities. If they are aware of their own shortcomings, they may begin to pick on others as a way of protecting themselves. Most children do not go after a child who appears to be stronger and more powerful.

Still other children tease without meaning. At age five, much of the teasing is in rhymes, which are fundamental parts of language development. Many children make up rhymes without thinking about the meaning. If you stop and ask why they are saying something mean about another child, they may not even realize that they are saying something hurtful.

If your child is teasing others, it is important to deal with it immediately. Make your values clear to your child. Although it is difficult for children to learn to be kind to others when much of what they are exposed to on television consists of insults or humiliations, it is extremely important that you relay your behavioral expectations to your child.

Talk to your child to see whether she can explain why she is teasing others. If her behavior is a way of expressing angry feelings, teach her more appropriate ways to express her anger.

If she thinks it is "funny" or a way of being accepted by other children, explain how hurtful teasing can be to another child. If necessary, speak to your child's teacher and engage her help in dealing with the behavior in school.

If your child is the one being teased, help her to come up with alternative responses to the teasing. Ignoring or possibly confronting the child alone are two possible alternative responses. Concentrate on how your child feels about the situation. Allow her to express her feelings to you and, in return, express your understanding and empathy. If necessary, role play with your child to help her practice alternative responses. While you play the role of your child, have your child pretend to be the teaser. When you have practiced several times, switch roles so your child can practice her own responses.

Although you can provide assistance to your child, it may still be necessary to intervene with either the classroom teacher or, in some cases, even the other child's parents. Some children are too uncomfortable or unable to handle the situation alone and need the help of an adult. If you have attempted to help your child deal with the teasing without success, first contact her classroom teacher to discuss the situation. Sometimes, a general discussion in the classroom about teasing is enough to put an end to it.

QUESTIONS AND ANSWERS

My husband and I have been having problems in our relationship for the past year and have decided to separate. Neither one of us wants to cause undue stress on our five year old. How do we explain things?

Separation and divorce are never easy subjects. It is important that you explain, in terms your child can understand, why you are separating. Children need to be reassured that they did not have anything to do with the situation and that there is nothing they can do to resolve it. Continue to make your child the top priority in your life, and provide constant reassurance of your love.

Help! My children, ages five and eight, seem to fight constantly. What can I do to gain a few minutes of peace in the house?

The fighting you are experiencing is quite common in most households. Try to find some cooperative activities for your children to work on together. Children are sometimes able to get along better if they are working toward a common goal. Try to provide each child with individual time with you. Often the fighting between siblings results from each one seeking the attention of their parents. If the fighting gets to be too much, separate your children for awhile. Have each find an activity to complete in separate areas of the house.

It seems as if all we hear are disturbing stories on the news. How do I help my five year old handle stories that may be particularly upsetting?

Some children have a remarkable ability to distance themselves from the disturbing information that is so commonplace today. Other childen are more easily frightened. Try to limit your child's exposure to news stories. Instead of watching the TV news early in the evening, wait until your child is in bed. Talk about the issues your child brings up. Don't assume that your child's concern is about a specific news story. Ask, in general terms, what's bothering him, and then respond from there.

After only two months of school, our five year old's teacher has expressed concern about her inability to keep up with the rest of the class. Should we be concerned so early in the school year?

Children need time to adjust to a new situation. If this is your child's first experience with school, she may need more time than a child who has already been in preschool. Arrange a conference with your child's teacher, and ask for specific examples of her inability to keep up. If you don't see the same difficulties at home or if it seems to be an adjustment problem, explain this to the teacher. Ask for specific suggestions of things you might be able to do at home to help your child. Arrange to meet with the teacher again in six or eight weeks to update your child's progress. If things haven't changed at that time, you may need to allow the school to intervene.

Although my child has been toilet trained since he was about three years old, he continues to have problems wetting the bed at night. He's almost five years old, and I'm not sure if I should be worried about it.

123

By age five, many, but not all children, are able to stay dry through the night. Before becoming overly concerned, here are a few suggestions. First, limit the amount of fluid intake after dinner. Make sure your child goes to the bathroom before going to bed. Before you go to bed at night, take him to the bathroom again. Some children sleep so soundly that they are not aware of the need to urinate. If your child wets the bed after you have taken him to the bathroom, set an alarm clock in his room to wake him in the middle of the night. If after you have tried these suggestions there is no change, you should consult your pediatrician.

Whenever my mother comes to visit she tends to "take over" my five year old. My daughter then disregards what I say if I reprimand her and looks to her grandmother for help.

Your mother's interactions with your daughter may be well-meaning but serve to undermine your authority with your child. It is important for you to speak with your mother, in private, about the problem. Try to explain the situation without accusing, and ask for your mother's help. Grandparents are often unaware of the effect they have when they interact with their grandchildren.

My five year old wants to sleep over at his friend's house. Is that too young?

Five and six year olds are often ambivalent about sleepovers. Spending the night away from Mom and Dad is a step toward autonomy, but it can also be a very anxiety-provoking situation. Give your child a say in the decision. If your child feels ready to try a sleepover, let him know you will be available if he needs you. Allow him to take a special blanket, stuffed animal, or other item from home that will help him feel more comfortable. If your child changes his mind at the last minute, assure him that it's okay. There will be other opportunities when he is more ready.

Although my child goes to bed without any difficulty, she's been waking up with nightmares the past few nights. What should I do?

Scary dreams are quite common among young children. They often occur more frequently during times of stress and illness or when there has been a traumatic event. When your child has a nightmare, offer immediate comfort. A calm voice and comforting touch often help your child get back to sleep. Explain that dreams are a normal part of everyone's sleep. Try not to analyze a nightmare or ask your child to recall what it was about. Most of the time children, as well as adults, forget the details of bad dreams. Asking your child to recall a nightmare will only make it real again.

Is it appropriate for a five year old to attend a funeral?

Most authorities on child development agree that five- and six-year-old children should be given a choice about attending the funeral of a family member or close friend. The reality of a funeral can be less troubling than the fantasies a child may have about what happens after death. Funerals also provide a framework that helps the child begin the grieving process. Additionally, it can also help children in their comprehension that death is final. If your child is apprehensive or uncertain about attending a funeral, don't force the issue. Take your child's lead in making a decision, and let him know he can always change his mind.

We will be moving to a new city in the next few months. How do I prepare my kindergartner for the move?

A move, like any loss, can be a challenge for a family. Because you have some time before the move, share as much information with your child as possible. Talk about the reasons for the move and how it will take place. Let your child ask questions and voice concerns. Allow your child to be in charge of some tasks. Stress can be reduced if your child feels she has some control. Plan a special farewell party, and try to celebrate your arrival at your new home. Try to involve your child's teacher in setting up pen pals.

GLOSSARY

Aggression behaviors that are intended to hurt someone, either physically or verbally.

Anger a temporary emotional state generally caused by frustration.

Articulation speech sound development.

Attention Deficit/Hyperactivity Disorder (ADHD) a primary difficulty maintaining a focus of attention. This often results in the disorganization of behavior as seen in inattention, impulsivity, or hyperactivity.

Cognitive Development the process by which we gain knowledge and become thinking beings.

Effective discipline the use of guidance and limits to teach the benefits of self-control.

Empathy the ability to experience something in the same way as another person.

Prejudice a judgment or opinion formed before the facts are known.

Psychostimulant medication medications used to treat ADHD. These work to increase the production of specific chemicals in the brain. The most common are Ritalin and Cylert.

Self-esteem a person's pride in himself; a feeling of worth and confidence.

Sight-word vocabulary words recognized on sight. This does not necessarily mean the reader understands the meaning of the word.

Speech dysfluency (stuttering) the repetition of sounds, syllables, or whole words while speaking.

Stereotypes generalities made about a group of people that are based on such characteristics as race, religion, nationality, or political beliefs.

Temperament a particular style of responding to the environment.

Time-out a quiet time away from any rewards, brought about by a child's inappropriate behavior. Time-out can also be used by parents when they need to calm down and regain control.

ADDITIONAL BOOKS AND RESOURCES FOR PARENTS

Books

Chess, S., and Thomas, A., *Know Your Child*. New York: Basic Books, 1987.

Clark, L., *The Time Out Solution—A Parent's Guide for Handling Everyday Behavior Problems*. Chicago: Contemporary Books, 1989.

Giarendi, R., *Back to the Family: How to Encourage Traditional Values in Complicated Times*. New York: Villard Books, 1990.

McNamara, B., and McNamara, F., *Keys to Parenting a Child with Attention Deficit Disorder*. Hauppauge, NY: Barron's Educational Series, 1993.

Parker, H., *The ADD Hyperactivity Workbook for Parents, Teachers, and Kids*. Plantation, FL: Impact Publishing, 1988.

Phelan, T., *1-2-3: Magic!* Glen Ellyn, IL: Thomas Phelan, 1984.

Schaefer, C., and DiGeronimo, T., *Teach Your Child to Behave*. New York: New American Library, 1990.

Sloane, H., *The Good Kid Book*. Champaign, IL: Research Press, 1988.

~~~~~~

Williamson, P., *Good Kids Bad Behavior—Helping Children Learn Self-Discipline.* New York: Simon & Schuster, 1990.

Zimbardo, P., and Radl, S., *The Shy Child: A Parent's Guide to Overcoming and Preventing Shyness from Infancy to Childhood.* New York: Doubleday/Dolphin, 1989.

Guides to Children's Reading

Notable Children's Books
American Library Association
50 East Huron Street
Chicago, IL 60611

Books for Children
Consumer Information Center
Dept. 116V
Pueblo, CO 81009

The Horn Book
The Horn Book, Inc.
31 St. James Avenue
Boston, MA 02116-4167

Guides to Videos and Computer Programs

Only the Best: The Guide to the Highest-Rated Educational Software, Preschool–Grade 12
(annual and cumulative editions)
Reed Reference Publishing
New Providence, NJ 07974

Choosing the Best in Children's Videos
American Library Association Video
50 East Huron Street
Chicago, IL 60611

Parents' Choice Magazine Guide to Video Cassettes for Children
Consumer Reports Books
Yonkers, NY 10703

Organizations

Big Brothers/Big Sisters of America
230 N 13th Street
Philadelphia, PA 19107
(215) 567-7880

CHADD   (Children and Adults with Attention Deficit Disorder)
499 Northwest 70th Avenue
Suite 308
Plantation, FL 33317
(305) 587-3700

ERIC Clearinghouse on Handicapped and Gifted Children
Council for Exceptional Children Information Center
1920 Association Drive
Reston, VA 22091
(703) 620-3660

Family Resource Coalition
200 S Michigan Avenue
Chicago, IL 60604
(312) 341-9361

National Association for the Education of Young Children
1834 Connecticut Avenue NW
Washington, DC 20009
(800) 424-2460

National Council for Children's Rights
220 Eye Street NE
Washington, DC 20002
(202) 547-6227

National Information Center for Children and Youths with
Handicaps (NICHCY)
PO Box 1492
Washington, DC 20012
(703) 893-6061

National Institute for Mental Health, Alcohol, Drug Abuse, and
Mental Health Administration
Park Lawn Building, 15C-05
5600 Fishers Lane
Rockville, MD 20857
(301) 443-4513 (publications)

ADDITIONAL BOOKS FOR CHILDREN

Ahlberg, J. Λ., *Starting School*. New York: Puffin Books, 1990.

Blume, J., *The Pain and the Great One*. New York: Dell Publishing, 1985.

Bourgeois, P., *Franklin Is Bossy*. New York: Scholastic, 1986.

Bourgeois, P., and Clark, B., *Franklin in the Dark*. New York: Scholastic, 1986.

Hazbry, N., and Conidy, R., *How to Get Rid of Bad Dreams*. New York: Scholastic, 1983.

Heine, H., *Friends*. New York: Macmillan, 1986.

Hoffman, M., *Amazing Grace*. New York: Scholastic, 1991.

Ives, S., Fassler, D., and Lash, M., *The Divorce Workbook: A Guide for Kids and Families*. Burlington, VT: Waterfront Books, 1985.

Mayer, M., *There's an Alligator Under My Bed*. New York: Dial Books for Young Readers, 1987.

Mayer, M., *There's a Nightmare in My Closet*. New York: Dial Books for Young Readers, 1976.

Moss, D., *Shelley, the Hyperactive Turtle*. Bethesda, MD: Woodbine House, 1989.

Pfister, M., *The Rainbow Fish*. New York: Scholastic. 1992.

Shapiro, L., *The Building Blocks of Self-Esteem*. King of Prussia, PA: Center for Applied Psychology, 1993.

Silverstein, S., *The Giving Tree*. New York: HarperCollins, 1964.

Stock, G., *The Kids Book of Questions*. New York: Workman, 1990.

Viorst, J., *Alexander and the Terrible, Horrible, No Good, Very Bad Day*. New York: Macmillan, 1972.

Viorst, J., *My Mama Says There Aren't Any Zombies, Ghosts, Vampires, Creatures, Demons, Monsters, Fiends, Goblins, or Things*. New York: Macmillan, 1973.

INDEX